I'm Tired of Waiting!

I'M TIRED
OF
WAITING!

Elisa Morgan

VICTOR BOOKS®
A Division of Scripture Press Publications Inc.

Scripture quotations are from the *Holy Bible, New International Version*
© 1973, 1978, 1984, International Bible Society. Used by permission of
Zondervan Bible Publishers.

Recommended Dewey Decimal Classification: 248.4
Suggested Subject Heading: CHRISTIAN BEHAVIOR

Library of Congress Catalog Card Number: 88-62867
ISBN: 0-89693-628-7

VICTOR BOOKS
A division of SP Publications, Inc.
Wheaton, Illinois 60187

Contents

DEDICATION

To Evan, Eva, and Ethan.
You
were worth the
wait!

1
WAITING
Why?

I wondered if God cared. When I prayed, nothing happened. No answers: yes, no . . . nothing.

So I waited, but I didn't wait very well. In fact, most of the time I was frustrated and angry—not exactly the contented version of godliness I kept telling myself I should resemble. My faith wavered. My temper flared. My energy ebbed. The present lost its value, and I lost my patience. But still, I waited.

During the four-and-one-half years my husband and I waited to receive a baby through adoption, I thought about this matter of waiting. When the doors of heaven are slammed shut, what can we do but sit on the doorstep and ponder our position?

Do you know what I realized? I hate to wait! I may force a smile and sit quietly, but on the inside I churn against delays. Since you're reading this book, I suspect that you're like me and millions of others who hate to wait!

The daily hassles of waiting for buses, for the washer to spin, the water to boil, the phone to ring, wrinkle our lives with frustration. In a way, we've come to expect such delays in the routine of life. We've all waited in line at the automatic teller machine, just to have it close when it's finally our turn. We sigh in exasperation, mumble a few words, get in our cars and go to another bank. We aren't stuck forever between living and nonliving just because a teller machine closes or the company is late or the line is busy.

Life's heavy waits hit us differently. They attack the very fiber of our being—our self-confidence and the values we ascribe to life and faith. There is something personal about waiting for a meaningful job. We feel singled out when we wait for a mate in a world of couples. Waiting for a baby, for a grown son to trust Christ, for another chance after we've seemingly ruined ourselves through failure—such times consume our contentment. We don't just grumble against them—we hate them!

WHY WE HATE TO WAIT

Two attitudes lie beneath our aversion to waiting. First, we see waiting as *inconvenient.* We've been weaned onto the drug of instant gratification and we aren't eager to give it up. We mail in ticket orders to save time in a line. We put our film in rush processing one day so we can pass snapshots around the next. We charge clothes, we rent appliances, finance cars and mortgage houses so that we can enjoy them today, not tomorrow.

Our generation is not alone in its fetish for the fast. It seems we're passing this preoccupation down to our young. Recent studies reveal that college students select careers largely on the basis of projected salary. Most opt for vocations which promise big bucks upon graduation rather than vesting an interest in work over the long haul.

We want what we want and we want it now. Christian songwriters Mary Rice and Wendy Hofheimer express our view of waiting in the song, "Instant Breakfast."

> Instant breakfast, instant life,
> Anything easy 'cuz that's what I like—
> Fast food places and banks with no lines,
> Anything easy, that will do fine.

Microwave oven—Mom's dream come true.
Put it on credit and take it with you.
Drive through carwash only $2.98,
Very convenient, the American Way.

Polaroid cameras, remote garage doors,
Instant coffee, K-Mart Stores,
Avon ladies right at your door,
Home computers, who could want more?

Instant Christian, changed overnight,
Anything easy 'cuz that's what we like.
Help me grow, Lord. Show me how.
Give me some patience. I want it now![1]

Second, we find waiting *humiliating*. It defines our status. In our society, those with power don't wait. There is an unwritten rule in many universities that students must wait ten minutes for an assistant professor who is late for class, twenty minutes for an associate professor and thirty minutes for a full professor. The appointment books of prominent lawyers and skilled physicians fill quickly and "waiting lists" contain names to be called in case of cancellation. Twenty bucks in the palm of a maitre d' gains access to a booked restaurant.

Dr. Robert Levine, professor of psychology at California State University, suggests a triad of power in the waiting game. "First, making a person wait is an exercise in power. Second, powerful people have the capacity to make others wait. And third, the willingness to wait acknowledges and legitimizes this power."[2]

There's something degrading about being put "on hold." It's okay if we're the ones punching the buttons; but when we're left listening to music on the other end of the line, we feel foolish.

We also find waiting humiliating because it implies our failure. People skirt the subject of our singleness, childlessness, or joblessness, not wanting to offend; and yet, behind their "kind" silence, we hear whispers of judgment.

We tend to believe their unspoken criticisms and, viewing our waiting days as wasted days, we often end up wasting even more time and energy. In the neither here-nor-there moments of waiting, it seems that nothing can be accomplished. We postpone buying a house and put off putting down roots. We assume we can't learn anything from the waiting process because nothing is happening. We think we can't enjoy life while we're in transition, because we're not where we want to be. Focusing only on the hope of the future, we mortgage the present. Victims of time, we sit on the back steps of life and watch it pass by.

Perhaps the most humiliating element of waiting is the way it highlights our helplessness. As we move toward our desires, we crash head-on into the obstacle of waiting. We pour out effort at work and see no results. We offer up prayers for a loved one's salvation and instead are allowed a closer view of his depravity. Waiting confronts us as an inflexible barrier blocking our path. In our age of self-sufficiency, helplessness is anything but attractive. We'd rather appear foolish than helpless. We'd rather be wrong than to wait.

SO WHY WAIT?

Since we find waiting both inconvenient and humiliating, why shouldn't we storm ahead, risk being wrong, and take what we want in life? Why wait?

Some of us don't. We find we can have what we want in some form now, so we rush ahead to enjoy.

Why wait to experience the bliss of sex in marriage? One in four sixteen-year-olds who regularly attend conservative churches have engaged in sexual intercourse.[3] The older a single person is, the more likely it is that he or she is experienced sexually. Why wait for the pleasure of sexual intimacy when it's readily available all around us?

Why not enjoy material goods now and defer payment? The Social Security Administration reports that only two percent of

Americans reach age sixty-five financially independent and eighty-five out of 100 Americans have less than $250 when they reach retirement age.[4] Further, the average American owes $1,600 in unpaid revolving credit; according to the Federal Reserve, we Americans carry more than $600 billion in consumer debt, not counting home mortgages. This is more than twice the debt level of 1981.[5] Why wait to live the good life when we can live it now and pay later?

Yes, there are those of us who rush ahead, stealing now what we might legitimately enjoy later, refusing to wait. Others of us see no way out of life but to wait, and so we waste our lives waiting. We berate our worth as individuals if we're educated but unemployed, available but unattached, fertile but childless. After failure, we rest our chins in the dirt and refuse to get up again. Playing the role of the victim, we make no effort to alleviate circumstances which are alterable.

Neither response to waiting is healthy. Neither honors ourselves or the God who made us. We don't call all the shots in life, but we aren't helpless victims of our circumstances either.

WAITING WELL

Why wait? Because when we wait, and wait well, we allow God to work.

Every year here in Colorado, we hear of folks who stray away from campsites, take solitary walks and end up lost in the Colorado Rockies. Mountain experts suggest one rule to follow in such cases: Sit down where you are and wait for someone to find you.

Now when you're lost, waiting is the last alternative on your list of solutions. You consider hiking up the mountain to the peak to get a better view of your surroundings. You contemplate walking down to the river and following it to civilization. You even imagine starting a fire and sending smoke signals. But sitting still? You've got to be kidding!

From an outsider's perspective, your waiting predicament looks completely different. Newscasters pass on descriptions of you to the public. Helicopters take off with wide search-lights. Family and friends organize search parties and thrash through the terrain. While you sit and wait, people are working to find you. With that larger picture in mind, waiting becomes your most practical option. If you're moving around, searchers won't be able to find you. If you sit and wait, their work will pay off.

From where we sit in the larger sphere of life, waiting often looks like humiliation, like failure, like helplessness. God's perspective is bigger. God views waiting as a purposeful part of life. It is a necessary pastime along the route to Christlike-ness. Once we come to grips with our inabilities, we can draw from God's abilities. Once we realize our need, He can fill it. Through waiting, we can learn patience, faith, trust, and utter reliance on His judgment. While we wait, God works.

In winter, trees stand bare and bleak against the gray sky and appear to be dead. We see the stark, leafless branches and assume that nothing is happening. Yet, nourishing fluids flow within the trees, supplying them with sustenance and life. Because we can't see within, we may miss this reality and its meaning.

Along these lines Helmut Thielicke once preached a famous sermon on the silence of God. In it he said,

Behind the silence are His higher thoughts.
He is fitting stone to stone
in His plan for the world and our lives,
even though we can only see a confused
and meaningless jumble of stones
heaped together under a silent heaven.[6]

There comes a time when you have to decide whether you're going to go with your impulses and run to the peaks, or follow the advice of experts and sit down to wait until someone finds you.

I hope you decide to wait, knowing that waiting well allows God to work. If you choose to wait, you can know that one day

14

your wait will end. You may have what you waited for. You may have something worse. You may have something better. But *you* will be better for having waited well.

2
WAITING
for God to Catch Up with You

G od can afford to be relaxed about time! He's eternal. He has all the time in the world. We don't! We are "like the new grass of the morning—though in the morning it springs up new, by evening it is dry and withered" (Psalm 90:5).

WAITING FOR A DAWDLING GOD

At times God seems unbearably slow, pokey, like a senile grandpa who tucked away special treats for all his grandchildren but can't remember just where he put them or which one is for whom; who dawdles through his days, chuckling at his absent-mindedness, enjoying each spontaneous moment as it passes.

■ We want to go.

"For I know the plans I have for you," declares the Lord, "plans to prosper you and not to harm you, plans to give you hope and a future" (Jeremiah 29:11). Reading this, we sigh, "Okay! Let's get on with them!"

At eighteen you planned to finish high school and then strike out on your own. After settling into a challenging and secure career, you envisioned marrying, having a few children, raising

17

them well, and then enjoying the fruits of your labors in the evening of your life. You hope to see your loved ones recover from illnesses and stick around to enjoy the good life.

So you set out along your predetermined path to godliness, checking in at preplanned rest stops along the way. You spend time with God each day, growing in your relationship with Him. You offer yourself in obedient efforts on His behalf.

■ God says no.

And then one day, your progress comes to a fast halt and you brace yourself for a sudden stop. Your mouth drops open as the familiar path to your goals is replaced by a twisting, turning road you don't recognize.

You did everything right, but there's no fulfilling job, no partner to share your hopes, dreams and failures. There's no child to mirror your image and ideals. There's no spot for your service.

Your children are uninterested in and unimpressed by God. Your parents edge closer to death each day, their health and mental awareness fading.

Perhaps we spend so much time waiting for God to catch up with us because we're erroneously convinced that we need to run ahead of Him in life. As a result, we take wrong turns. We get tired. We faint. We fail.

Step by step, we calculate what will get us where we want to be. But the truth is that we don't know. Sometimes the only path toward godliness is through the desert. God detours us off the main road in order to take us where we need to be.

DETOUR: LESSONS FROM THE DESERT

He sat by a well. It had been a long and dangerous trip. He was middle-aged now, yet still his face was a jagged version of handsomeness which commands a second look. He sat by the well, cupping his face in muscular hands as he thought back.

He had lived in Pharaoh's courts for forty years, riding through the land in his own horse-drawn carriage, floating the Nile in a golden barge, waited upon by eager-to-please servant girls. He remembered his university days at the Temple of the Sun, the Oxford of its day. He'd stood hands above the average scholar in his ability to argue philosophy and compute figures.

He could have been Pharaoh! He could have held the highest office in the land! As the adopted son of the Pharaoh's daughter, Moses had been offered the job on three different occasions. He was twenty when his grandfather died and the throne was first offered to him. He'd refused. His mother had a half brother who became Pharaoh. He died five years later. Again, at twenty-five, Moses was offered the job and again, he declined. His mother married another half brother who served as Pharaoh and jealously opposed Moses. But Moses wasn't interested in being king. At age forty, Moses turned down the opportunity to be Pharaoh for the last time when he fled Egypt for Midian.

Now he sat by a well, puzzling. This was not what he'd planned. He'd dreamed of delivering the Israelites. That had been his ambition for as long as he'd remembered. He wasn't sure just when the promptings began. When he was three months old, his mother left him in the reeds of the Nile, carefully planning for his discovery by the Pharaoh's daughter. Because the Israelites were growing too numerous in proportion to the slave owners, the Pharaoh had decreed that all male children be put to death. Moses was discovered in the reeds by the Pharaoh's daughter who raised him as her own son. Miraculously, his own mother was hired to nurse him; because Moses lived with his natural parents for the first few years of his life, he heard often of his real heritage.

Perhaps, as the historian Josephus writes, Moses' father had a dream in which the future of Moses was revealed to him and he shared it with his son. However it occurred, Moses knew early in his life that he was a Hebrew; while he received the benefits of being raised an Egyptian, he remained true to his people in his heart.

■ The crash plan.

Moses was a man with a mission. Fervently he went about the

fulfillment of his mission. With his eyes fixed on his goal, he plowed ahead. Moses observed an Egyptian beating a Hebrew and defended his kinsman by killing the Egyptian. The next day, seeing two Hebrews fighting, he intervened and was challenged, "Who made you ruler and judge over us? Are you thinking of killing me as you killed the Egyptian?" (Exodus 2:14)

While he could top anybody in being an Egyptian, Moses was on the bottom rung in being a Hebrew. While he knew how to conduct himself under his own control, he knew little about how to submit himself under God's control. Consequently, when he saw the Egyptians oppressing the Israelites, he blew it. He had the right goal, but pursued it from the wrong path.

When Pharaoh heard of Moses' mistake, Moses fled to Midian and there sat by a well until he met his future wife and sisters-in-law from the sheepherding family of Jethro. In naming his son Gershom, meaning "I have become an alien in a foreign land," Moses expressed his deep sense of abandonment and exile.

People with a mission for God often find themselves in need of further training to carry it out. We who have dreams of pursuing specific goals may discover ourselves stopped in our tracks and directed down an obscure path. We who run after goals, believing them to be in God's will and honoring to Him, may find ourselves detoured over the dry path of the desert. It's not a road we would have chosen for ourselves.

■ The Master's plan.
Desert paths have much to teach, for it is on their terrain that we learn lessons we can learn nowhere else.

Following his escape to Midian, Moses spent the next forty years learning dependency on God. His assignment was the tending of the sheep of his father-in-law. His library was the land. His tablet was his heart. His pencil was the finger of God.

Each time he heard of the suffering Hebrews, he bucked against his isolation. He struggled with God. Guilt haunted his

20

days, twisting its ugly accusations through his thoughts. "You're worthless! You'll always be worthless!"

Moses put one foot in front of the other and determined he would pass down this path and somehow get back in sight of his goal again. To his surprise, he found the desert dust to be a great teacher. The desert taught Moses several life-changing lessons.

● Willing participation. God may slow us down and detour us off our secure path, but we won't learn anything unless we apply ourselves to the new course set before us.

Moses "refused to be known as the son of Pharaoh's daughter. He chose to be mistreated along with the people of God rather than to enjoy the pleasures of sin for a short time. He regarded disgrace for the sake of Christ as of greater value than the treasures of Egypt" (Hebrews 11:24-26).

Moses could have avoided the path of the desert. If he had made an appeal to the princess, she perhaps would have subdued the anger of the Pharaoh against him. On the other hand, he could have offered physical presence but mental and emotional absence to the lessons of the desert. We all know what it's like to go through the motions without putting our hearts in the process.

Moses chose neither of these options. When he found a spot of safety and service with Jethro and his daughters, he applied himself to learning the lessons of the desert.

How do we respond when we are given a similar opportunity to draw away from a place of significance and opportunity to sit and learn hard lessons in a dry desert? In his book, *Don't Waste Your Sorrows*, Paul Billheimer points out, "It is not always the character of the affliction which determines its spiritual value but rather the length of its continuation and one's reaction to it."[1]

Chuck Swindoll also drives home the need for us to accept the manner in which God schools His children.

Moses had been driven out of Egypt with broken dreams. He sat down with a box of medals from all his achievements in Egypt and knew everything was down the tubes . . . but we don't linger often on Moses at the well. We immediately rush him to the burning bush and on to the Exodus. In real life, we must be willing to stay at the well as long as God wants us to.[2]

● Answers from a silent God. Over his shoulder, Moses searched for a glimpse of God. He begged for directions. But, as in all deserts—as in all times of waiting—he found aloneness to be a part of the course.

In a desert of grief after the death of his wife, C.S. Lewis wrote,

> Meanwhile, where is God? This is one of the most disquieting symptoms. When you are happy, so happy that you have no sense of needing Him, so happy you are tempted to feel His claims upon you as an interruption, if you remember yourself and turn to Him with gratitude and praise, you will be—or so it feels—welcomed with open arms. But go to Him when your need is desperate, when all other help is vain, and what do you find? A door slammed in your face, and a sound of bolting and double-bolting on the inside. After that, silence. . . . Why is He so present a commander in our time of prosperity and so very absent a help in our time of trouble?[3]

Just when he thought he would perish on this dry path, Moses began to grasp the message of his "absent" kind of professor. As Frederick Buechner puts it, "It is out of the absence of God that God makes Himself present. . . . God doesn't always give answers. He gives Himself."[4]

Moses wasn't told exactly when he would go to deliver the Israelites. He wasn't given a glimpse of how they would be freed. In the forty years he wandered the desert, he heard of their increased bondage. God gave him no answers, but Moses met God.

In Hebrews 11:27, we're told that Moses persevered

because "he saw Him who is invisible." The strength Moses would demonstrate later in his life, the ability to wait on God's timing, the wise leadership over the flock of Israel, these things Moses would handle well because of what he found in the desert—not answers to his every question, but a God who could fill his every lack.

To his surprise, God wasn't dawdling way back behind him, but was in front of him leading him step by step. He was beside him, lifting each foot to move it ahead. He came after him to whisper reminders of the progress he'd already made. He surrounded him with encouragement and drew him on.

● Good, better, best. Moses, a man of high degrees, knew he needed more education. Even one who has received the finest education his country has to offer has more to learn at the feet of God. You've probably discovered that qualities like humility, submission, faith, perseverance and dependence on God aren't acquired during fat periods of life. While fitting securely into schedules that run according to our orders, we don't learn to follow another.

Instead, it's during the lean years of inactivity, of questioning, of waiting, that such qualities are discovered and possessed. When we're caught up short by circumstances and are forced to face our inabilities, we learn to depend upon God's abilities. Our best can be made better by God.

Just when we think we understand how God works, He changes His methods in our lives. Just when we think we can keep Him boxed in and under our control, He breaks out to be God to us again.

● Preparation through separation. Bible scholar F.B. Meyer acknowledges Moses' potential while underlining his need for development. While there was "the making of a saint in him," Meyer writes, it would take long years of waiting and trials before "this strong and self-reliant nature could be broken down and shaped into a vessel meet for the Master's use."[5]

We may find ourselves shelved for a time, doing something we consider unimportant and separated from the real business of life. In the adjustment period after a move, when old friends are a long-distance call away, I've felt like the only friend I can chat with is myself as I unpack box after box in loneliness. In the exhausting days of being a young mother, up all night and interrupted all day, it was easy to wonder how much my life was worth. Stuck in a sickbed, staring at a white ceiling, I've questioned God's wisdom in pushing me aside to such a time of apparent waste.

Yet, it's during the lonely unpacking after a move that I acquire a sensitivity to others who are lonely. It's in the long nights of walking a baby that I learn the patience for dealing with teenagers. It's when I am flat on my back, helpless to aid another, that I come to grips with my need for God.

> When God lovingly draws us into a dark night of the soul, there is often a temptation to blame everyone and everything for our inner dullness and to seek release from it. The preacher is such a bore. The hymn singing is so weak. We may begin to look around for another church or a new experience to give us "spiritual goose bumps." That is a serious mistake. Recognize the dark night for what it is. Be grateful that God is lovingly drawing you away from every distraction so that you can see Him. Rather than chafing and fighting, become still and wait.[6]

Preparation often comes through separation. When we're busy living our lives on our schedules, we may miss the lessons God wants to teach.

● Gaining vision. In the blackest of times, we want to give up. In the driest deserts, we want to quit. Moses learned to look for God's face in the dust of the desert. When he was tempted to lose hope that God would use him to deliver the Israelites, he clung to God.

How we love control! On Tuesday we'll do the wash, on Friday we'll get the groceries, and on Saturday we'll do the lawn. It's frustrating when our schedules are interrupted and our plans ruined. We buck and swerve like a bronc with an unwanted burden on its back. When God takes us aside and rearranges our plans, we rebel.

Moses learned that before you can gain a vision for what God can do through you, you must gain a vision for God. In desert experiences, we are stripped of all that we cling to for comfort, of all that prevents us from experiencing utter dependency on God.

THE SHORTEST DISTANCE BETWEEN TWO POINTS

It took Moses forty years, but he completed his course in the desert and returned to a spot where he not only saw his dreams promised again but went on to see them realized. The shortest distance between two points is not always a straight line. Sometimes, the only path toward our goals in life, toward godliness, detours off alone through the desert. Ruth Harms Calkin's words echo the lessons of the desert.

Thank You For Waiting

Had You given in to me, Lord,
On the thing I wanted so much,
My life today
Would be a sorry mess.

I tell You nothing new—
I simply repeat
What You told me
Long, long ago.

Finally today I see it—
From Your point of view.
Thank You for not giving in to me.

Thank You most of all
For patiently waiting
For me to give in to You.[7]

25

Perhaps we're not waiting for God to catch up with us so much as He is waiting for us to catch up with Him. He knows the plans He has for us, and the path which will lead us to them. Don't bother looking over your shoulder. God is up ahead!

3
WAITING
for a Job

He padded down the walk, stooped to pick up the paper, and headed back inside. The coffee was ready. Wincing as the rubber band snapped against his finger, he uncurled the paper and pulled out the want ads. He put on his glasses, and began at the beginning.

It had been six months. Six months of circling hopeful leads and following them up with phone calls which had left him feeling humiliated and frustrated. They should be called the unwanted ads.

He'd prepared a ream of resumés and scattered them across the city to agencies that said they'd be in touch. A few companies sounded interested and said they might call. Most filed his application with fifty others and forgot him.

Between jobs. Fired. Laid off. Terminated. Let go. No longer needed. Unemployed. However you describe it, the experience of being without work stings.

WORKING NINE TO FIVE

Working is almost as basic to humans as breathing. From our days in the Garden when we were assigned to care for creation, we've had work to do.

Whether the hours are nine to five or eleven to seven, people all over the globe spend an average of 125,000 working hours in a lifetime. Some work because they enjoy it, some because it gets them out of the house, others because they feel they're called by God. Most work for a paycheck.

Solomon suggests an even more fundamental reason for working. "Then I realized that it is good and proper for a man to eat and drink, and to find satisfaction in his toilsome labor under the sun during the few days of life God has given him—for this is his lot" (Ecclesiastes 5:18).

In order to provide us with meaning for our days and a niche in His sovereign purpose for the universe, God gave us work. Because of sin and its resulting curse, the pure joy of work is now dampened with sweat. No longer are we able to merely work; now we also toil. But even in our toil, we know that God thoughtfully provided work to fill our days with meaningful activity.

If work is a gift from God, why then do we sometimes find ourselves waiting for work? We've taken the courses, positioned the right letters after our names, and dressed for success; yet all we can find is a job flipping burgers or checking dry cleaning. And sometimes not even that.

WAITING FOR THE WANT ADS

Wherever it hits us, waiting for work is an awkward time.

You're fresh out of college, pumped with idealism and high hopes. After four months of searching for the perfect job, you realize you'll have to lower your gaze in order to pay the rent.

You've been with a company for five years but want to make a career change. You quit, thinking something will open up right away, but it doesn't.

Your secure job becomes insecure, and after a few months of limbo, you're let go. You had just achieved seniority and now you'll have to begin at the bottom again, if someone will give you a chance.

When we're waiting for work, our hours hang loosely on our

days, void of meaning and purpose.

■ Down and doubters.

For some of us, waiting for work is a time of panic. "How will I pay the bills? What if my house is foreclosed? What if I have an emergency? What was all my schooling for?"

For others the questions dig deeper, hacking against the dry rock of doubt. "What's the purpose of life? Who am I anyway? What good am I? What good is God?"

Sitting on the sloping back of a question mark, we precariously balance our desire to die with our will to live.

■ Hope deferred.

Waiting for work unravels the four-ply chord of our personhood. First, it frazzles our *emotions*. "Hope deferred makes the heart sick" (Proverbs 13:12).

Among the 140,000 unemployed Coloradans in 1987 was Baxter Stovall. A staff writer for the *Rocky Mountain News* described Stovall's plight as emotionally crippling.

> Junkyard or graveyard, it didn't matter. Because Baxter Stovall had fallen into one, he was flirting with the other. He had a bad back, and nobody would hire him, and he was considering suicide. . . . Without hope, a man's hands can freeze into fists.[1]

Slipping in and out of depression, we fight to bolster our egos for an upcoming interview. We hide our inadequacies behind a facade of self-pride only to slither home in shambles when the appointment passes without results.

Second, waiting for work wears on our *relations*. It unties the ties that bind. Friends and family who stood alongside us as we launched our dreams now wonder if we'll ever grow up and become productive. Mates who've supported with prayer, pep talks, and patience lean under the extra load. Roles are altered and sometimes reversed when the primary breadwinner becomes just another breadeater. Children who've bravely believed Mom or Dad will come out on top begin to go under.

Ironically, we seem to hurt most those we love the best.

We allow them to enter our tortured world and then we turn against them. Defensively, we push away those we really want to draw closer.

Third, waiting for work shreds our *identity*. Without work, we're not sure who we are anymore. Tom Horsman had worked nineteen years for Frontier Airlines when the company folded. He hasn't worked a day since. Just a month after Frontier failed, Horsman's stomach rebelled. Because he couldn't keep food down, he dropped from 145 to 105 pounds. Later, his legs quit working and he became dependent on an aluminum walker for mobility. He candidly admits,

> I know exactly what caused it. It was the trauma of working all those years and then it's gone. After a while you think of having a job for life. This is you. This is your place. You're proud of what you do.
>
> You grow old with a company. I just turned forty-six and was twenty-six when I started. I didn't know the front of a plane from the behind but people taught me and I learned. I was good at what I did.[2]

Our work defines our identity. When we're good at what we do, we feel even better about ourselves. But when we're forced to wait for work, we wonder who we are.

Last, this time of waiting frays our *spirits*. It tears us away from God. Even when we turn to Him for help, we hear for the umpteenth time, "I'm sorry. There are no openings at the present. Please check back in a few weeks." We're emotionally, relationally, personally, and now, spiritually undone.

Settling into apathy, we check out. Why make the bed? Why mess with church? Why not watch more TV, eat all we can stomach, stay up late, drink, charge it, let loose our tongues? God doesn't care, so why should we?

But checking out isn't the only option for the paycheckless in life. While surveying unemployed workers in the Detroit area, University of Michigan Researcher Louis Ferman found one man who remained resilient through his battle with unemployment. He'd been laid off in 1962 when the Studebaker Corporation was close to folding, again by a truck manufacturer that went bankrupt in the 1970s, and a third time during the Chrysler cutbacks in the early 1980s. Ferman expected him to be a "basket case" but instead found him to be among the best adjusted of all those he'd interviewed. Asked his secret, the man said, "I've got a loving wife and I go to church every Sunday."[3]

A loving wife and a commitment to a local body of believers. This man found a niche of value for himself in the everyday structures of his life. While without work, he occupied his time and thoughts with faithfulness in the place where he was.

The Bible tells of a man who was trained to serve in a specific spot and then was held back from possessing that position. While he waited for an opening, David applied himself to the job he'd already been given. God gave him the assignment to grow in godliness through obedience and he bent his back to the task. In his wait for work, we find help for ours.

A KING WITHOUT A CROWN

From shepherd to second-in-command. In the space of a few unexpected moments, the sixteen-year-old, youngest son of Jesse became the future king of Israel. The nation's first king, Saul, had lost God's favor due to disobedience. While Saul wasn't ready to give up the throne, God was ready to choose a replacement. So the Prophet Samuel headed out to Bethlehem to anoint the one whose heart had been prepared to serve. His name was David.

There were fourteen long years between anointing and coronation. For fourteen years David herded sheep, served folks who should have served him, fled from enemies he could have killed, and wrestled with God's power to avenge. For fourteen years, David was a king without a crown, waiting for his coronation day.

In the first months of his new identity, David wavered between excitement and exasperation. Pronounced royal one day and summoned to the palace to serve the king the next, he wasn't sure where he stood. Even after demonstrating his loyalty to his country through slaying its chief enemy—the Philistine monster, Goliath—David's anxiety continued. He replaced the slain giant as the enemy in Saul's mind and for the next decade, David found himself scrambling over the countryside as in guerrilla warfare, hiding from Saul.

As the king-elect, he belonged in the palace, not in the pasture. But between anointing and coronation comes the test of waiting in obedience. Between knowing what we'd like to get out of life and getting it comes a time when we must learn to obey God in the spot where we are.

While he was anointed as king at sixteen years of age, David was thirty when he was crowned. Over a period of fourteen years, David learned what it meant to love and serve God through the obedience of waiting on Him. Threaded through his story are the principles of obedience which made his wait worthwhile.

■ David was obedient when nobody was watching. David did what he was supposed to do, whether or not he had an audience. He strove for excellence in the mundane routine of life. In fact, he was almost forgotten in the process. When Samuel went to Bethlehem to anoint one of Jesse's sons as king of Israel, David wasn't even called into the room. So sure were they that it would be the handsome Eliab, they didn't consider the rest of the boys. God had some powerful words to say on this point: "Do not consider his appearance or his height, for I have rejected him. The Lord does not look at the things man looks at. Man looks at the outward appearance, but the Lord looks at the heart" (1 Samuel 16:7).

When asked if he had any other sons, Jesse replied, "There is still the youngest, but he is tending the sheep," as if to say, "He doesn't even know how to tie his shoes yet." At that point, Samuel beckoned David and, hearing the Holy Spirit's confirmation, promptly anointed him king.

Though no one watched, David obeyed. He went about the tasks of his day as though the destiny of the earth depended on their proper completion. His father had assigned him to tend the sheep, so he tended them.

David didn't just agree to tend his father's flock; he spent himself in the effort. If he had to be a shepherd, he'd be an excellent one. When David approached Saul with his credentials for fighting Goliath, he said, "Your servant has been keeping his father's sheep. When a lion or a bear came and carried off a sheep from the flock, I went after it, struck it and rescued the sheep from its mouth. When it turned on me, I seized it by its hair, struck it and killed it" (1 Samuel 17:34-35).

I don't know about you, but I would have seriously considered letting that one sheep go! What's one sheep? But David was convinced that we honor God when we obey fully in any situation, no matter how seemingly unimportant. David remembered what most of us forget—God won't overlook us when we're obedient in the everyday. When we're waiting for something, we usually look beyond the present toward the future and what we desire. We barely recognize the opportunity of today because we're so focused on the next day or the next.

God won't overlook us for something special because we were stuck in the mundaneness of obedience in the everyday. He won't call our name when we're out of the room. When we apply ourselves to obeying Him, no matter where we are, no matter how fulfilling or how disappointing, we'll find ourselves rewarded for our wait. It is when we're carving out a groove of obedience that we honor God and prepare ourselves for the future He has designed.

David also knew that God doesn't waste even a minute of our lives. He'll use all that we do and all that we learn to do. David never dreamed that his shepherding skills would be valuable anywhere but in the pastures of Bethlehem. And yet, the years he tended the sheep of his earthly father trained him to care for the sheep of his Heavenly Father.

When David composed Psalm 23, he conveyed a shepherd's understanding of life with sheep. But he also etched out a wise king's vision of how God leads His human flock.

The Lord is my shepherd,
I shall lack nothing.
He makes me lie down in green pastures,
He leads me beside quiet waters,
He restores my soul.
He guides me in paths of righteousness
for His name's sake.
Even though I walk through the valley
of the shadow of death,
I will fear no evil,
for You are with me;
Your rod and Your staff,
they comfort me.

You prepare a table before me
in the presence of my enemies
You anoint my head with oil;
my cup overflows.
Surely goodness and love will follow me
all the days of my life,
and I will dwell in the house of the Lord
forever.

When I was sixteen, I worked as a salesclerk in a jewelry store. I also took typing at school. My mom made me. I'd rather have finished class an hour earlier and pocketed an extra hour of minimum wage, but my mom directed me to typing class and declared it a nonnegotiable.

At 2:00 on Friday afternoon, plunking away at a mean forty-five words a minute (with fifteen mistakes), I'd stare at the clock and wait for the bell. Typing seemed a meaningless way to get through the day.

I never dreamed that eight years later I'd be working my way through seminary by typing admittal forms for hospital patients. I never imagined that ten and even fifteen years later I'd be sitting at a computer writing radio scripts, articles for magazines, and books. I never expected to use what I labeled "a holding pattern skill" in service for God.

What skills are you currently learning which God may one day use for your benefit and His glory? The conversational skills from the only job you can find—waitressing? The listening abilities you gain as a parent, stuck at home reading want ads? The organizational skills from volunteer projects you select to pass the hours?

God won't waste what we learn. He won't overlook us while we're busy obeying Him in the everyday. When we apply ourselves in the here and now, we allow God to use us while we wait and then again later when we get where He wants us to be.

God desires obedience of you in your wait. Nothing is too small to be done wholeheartedly for Him. And where you sit in your seeming smallness, God will find you when it's time to move. "And whatever you do, work at it with all your heart, as working for the Lord" (Colossians 3:23).

■ David was obedient when playing second fiddle.
David humbled himself and served others when he could have been served. Transition times can be among the most frustrating times of life. When we're forced to learn the ropes of living between jobs, we can end up feeling like hanging ourselves on them.

In 1 Samuel 16:14-23, we read that David was summoned to soothe the ebbing sanity of Saul by playing his harp. From the dryness of his daily routine caring for sheep, David was plunged into royalty. At first he was awed. When the newness wore off, he was disappointed.

Here was a man, committed to serving God in the mundane, face-to-face with a king who refused to bow down to Him in the spectacular. Where David thought he would receive training and perhaps respect as a king-elect, he was treated as a servant and witnessed some family scenes of mental anguish.

But he didn't buckle under. David pricked up his ears and applied himself to gleaning whatever he could from Saul. He obediently humbled himself and served. For a time, before Saul's jealousy was ignited against David, David had the opportunity to learn firsthand what court life was all about. He spent his time going back and forth between serving Saul and serving sheep, and in this unlikely combination, he developed kingly skills.

● Your wife makes more money as a part-time secretary than you bring home from five temporary assignments a month.

● You've been trained to run a plant, and the only work you can find is as a machinist.

● In order to be available when the kids get home from school, you take a job that pays minimum wage when you could earn double at a full-time position.

Even in such humbling hollows of waiting, there is a role to be fulfilled. Playing second fiddle is marvelous training for solo performances. Waiting for work, we may be asked to serve when we have the ability and qualifications to lead.

■ David was obedient when the pressure was on.

David refused to compromise when the stakes were high. Chapters 19–31 of 1 Samuel deal with Saul's pursuit of David and David's fleeing from Saul. On two separate occasions, David had the opportunity to kill Saul and to claim his crown at last. In both instances, he refused to compromise his commitment to God's timing. David chose to be patient, to wait for God to avenge his right to the throne.

The first situation is recorded in 1 Samuel 24:1-22. Unknown to Saul, David and his men were hiding in a cave. When Saul entered the same cave, David could have caught him and killed him. He didn't. The second instance is recorded in 1 Samuel 26. David crept into Saul's camp at night but rather than killing him, took his spear and water jug which had been placed by his head. He then went to the outskirts of the camp and yelled back to Saul that he had spared his life once again.

The word *patience* describes a stable man who is standing still and erect while the wind howls all around him. It contrasts with *perseverance* which pictures a man straining ahead and pushing through the wind to reach his goal. When the pressure was on, David patiently waited on God. He stood firmly

against the winds that demanded compromise. While he could
have ended his wait by seizing the throne for himself, he chose
instead to rely on God's sovereign timing in his life.

How great is the temptation to take control! When we're
waiting for work, we'd do most anything to end the wait. The
hours, the location, the pay, even the legality of a job cease to
matter, when we're desperate to provide the basics.

While I believe that God will let us assume command of our
lives when we insist upon having it, I'm also convinced that we
don't know best how to meet our needs. David realized that
God's timing would make sense in the long run. He let go of
the temptation to assume command over God and took hold of
the certainty that God would, in time, crown him. Take a look
at some words he wrote during those fugitive days.

> Have mercy on me, O God, have mercy on me,
> for in You my soul takes refuge.
> I will take refuge in the shadow of Your wings
> until the disaster has passed.
> I cry out to God Most High, to God,
> who fulfills His purpose for me,
> rebuking those who hotly pursue me;
> God sends His love and faithfulness (Psalm 57).

> Deliver me from my enemies, O God;
> protect me from those who rise up against me.
> Deliver me from evil-doers
> and save me from bloodthirsty men. . . .
> They return at evening, snarling like dogs,
> and prowl about the city.
> They wander about for food and howl if not satisfied.
> But I will sing of Your strength,
> in the morning I will sing of Your love;
> for you are my fortress,
> my refuge in times of trouble (Psalm 59).

> Do not fret because of evil men

or be envious of those who do wrong;
for like the grass they will soon wither,
like green plants they will soon die away. . . .
Commit your way to the Lord;
trust in Him and He will do this:
He will make your righteousness shine like the dawn,
the justice of your cause like the noonday sun.
Be still before the Lord and wait patiently for Him;
do not fret when men succeed in their ways,
when they carry out their wicked schemes . . .
for evil men will be cut off,
but those who hope in the Lord will inherit the land
(Psalm 37)

When the pressure's on, wait obediently on God to resolve your conflicts.

■ David was obedient when the chips were down.
After he'd stumbled in his faith, David got back up on his feet and tried again. His waiting wasn't all success. He stubbed his toe on his doubts and landed, sprawled on his face, in the dirt.

In 1 Samuel 21 and 27, we see David relying on deception rather than divine inspiration to get him through some rough spots. Hounded by Saul for months, he lied, faked insanity, and led raids on enemies of Israel while disguising himself as a servant of the Philistine king. The more he was afraid of Saul, the more he lied. The more he lied, the more he was afraid of Saul.

We've been there. We've sat with our hopes crushed and our dreams dying. We've talked to God and found our prayers bouncing back at us from the ceiling. We've despaired under the seeming absence of God until our doubts grew deeper than the reservoirs of our faith.

David didn't sit forever with his chin in the dirt of his doubts. Psalm 34 proceeds from his questions and illustrates how David came out of his depression and failure. Read what he wrote as he wrestled with his wait and with his unswerving commitment to keep God in control of it.

I sought the Lord and He answered me;
He delivered me from all my fears.
Those who look to Him are radiant;
their faces are never covered with shame. . . .
The angel of the Lord encamps around those
who fear Him, and He delivers them.
Taste and see that the Lord is good;
blessed is the man who takes refuge in Him.
Fear the Lord, you His saints,
for those who fear Him lack nothing.
The lions may grow weak and hungry,
but those who seek the Lord lack no good thing. . . .
The Lord redeems His servants;
no one who takes refuge in Him will be condemned.

David, anointed as king but not crowned, says, "Those who seek the Lord lack no good thing." Wow! Out of the dust of his doubts came the fulfillment of his faith. David obediently got back up and plodded on in his waiting.

FOLDED HANDS OR QUICK FEET?

Oswald Chambers wrote these words in his classic devotional, *My Utmost for His Highest:*

Wait on God and He will work,
but don't wait in spiritual sulks
because you cannot see an inch in front of you!
To wait is not to sit with folded hands,
but to learn to do what we are told.[4]

David waited fourteen years between anointing and coronation. He was obedient when no one was watching, even when he was playing second fiddle. He was obedient when the pressure was on and the stakes were high and also when the chips were down after he'd fallen into failure.

Between a king and his crown, between anointing and coronation, comes the test of obedience in waiting. Resist the urge to play hooky from the job you've been given. When you're waiting for the work you want, apply yourself to the vocation of obedience. Don't fold your hands. Do what you're told.

4
WAITING
for a Mate

Y ou want to be married and you've claimed Psalm 37:4 "The Lord will give you the desires of your heart" on thirty-seven separate occasions. You've pumped and primped, had your colors done, developed conversational skills, pursued a career and frequented all the "right" spots. Across your forehead is stamped, "ELIGIBLE, TALENTED, COMPASSIONATE, CAPABLE MATE." And still, your nights are spent alone.

READY TO WED

There are very few single people who decide one day that they will never marry. Most are single because for them, marriage has never been an option.

Aside from the struggles with sex, loneliness, isolation and the financial problems, what's so tough about being single? If you're unmarried, you know. Most folks who are single find themselves waiting for the altar and for real life to begin. Three perspectives on singleness shape our thinking.

■ Flunking "Adulthood 101."

Singleness is seen as abnormal in our society. Suburban homes with two-car garages house two people and their two children.

Only the freakish, forlorn, or fickle stop short of the altar.

Developmental psychologists list "selecting a mate," "learning to live with a mate," "starting a family," and "rearing a family" among the major developmental tasks of adulthood.[1] Those who aren't married can't help wondering if they've flunked adulthood.

■ Neither here nor there.

Singleness is seen as limbo. It's the state of transition, of being neither here nor there. Women wonder about pursuing careers which might make them intimidating to available men. Men contemplate heavy work schedules which might take them out of the mainstream of dating. Both tend to put off investing in homes and furnishings.

The Chicago *Tribune* carried a story about a single woman named Donna, which points out the neither-here-nor-there aspect of singleness.

> There's no reason to believe she'll be moving out soon. No job transfer looming. No windfall on the way for a down payment on a house. But despite the fact that Donna's immediate future seems to be right there in that Old Town one-bedroom, the corner of the dining room is piled with boxes. Cartons filled with books, with Pyrex, with things she doesn't need right away but figures she will someday. . . . She believes that sooner or later a man will enter her life and take her away from her Old Town apartment. . . . They will set up a home together. That will be her real home. They will use the Pyrex together.[2]

■ Undelivered heart's desire.

Aside from being seen as abnormal and temporary, singleness is, thirdly, seen as deprivation. In her book, *Reflections for Women Alone*, Carole Streeter writes, "We live with the tension of not having what we think we want—a husband, a shared home. We wonder if we don't matter very much because we don't have what we think we should have, what we felt was promised by someone."[3]

The verse says, "Delight yourself in the Lord and He will give you the desires of your heart." We know what we want! When we go to God in obedience and "delight ourselves in Him," we expect delivery!

Seeing singleness as abnormal or as deprivation warps our understanding of it. For some, it is not a time of waiting at all but rather of living fully here and now. For others, it is a time of anticipation, of submission to God and to His ways.

SO WHY AREN'T YOU MARRIED?

"So why aren't you married?" It's probably the question most often asked of singles. Why, indeed. Most singles would like to know themselves. Rhena Taylor was a missionary in Kenya. She was asked the question, "So why aren't you married?" so many times that she developed this thoughtful response.

If you are a Christian who sincerely wants the will of God in your life, then you are not single (or alone) because you:
    —went to a women's teachers' training college;
    —belong to the war generation;
    —are unattractive and perhaps too strong-willed;
    —are confined to your home looking after your parents;
    —never met any men;
    —have had your partner cruelly taken away by God.
(To reflect the man's perspective, I might add:
    —had a mother who never cut the apron strings;
    —struggle with shyness;
    —never made a success of yourself in a career;
    —have an unrealistic checklist for a perfect partner.)
You are single because it is God's calling and choice for you at this time. His chosen ministry for you now is that of a single person.[4]

Rather than being abnormal, singleness can be a calling.

Waiting for a mate, like waiting for other things in life, is a timely challenge used by God for our growth.

■ Singled out.

I went through most of my days in seminary as a single person. Of the ten women I entered with, only one shared my degree program. Most of the men were married, but there were enough single males around to keep me busy. Distracted. Confused. Ready to wed.

After a year of dating men destined for the pulpit, the mission field, the therapist's chair, and youth work, I was confused as to what I wanted in a mate. What God wanted for me seemed even foggier.

One morning as I made my bed, I was mulling over my recent options. Unsatisfied with any of them and yet fearful of casting them aside too quickly, God brought a thought to me. "Separate thyself unto Me," I heard in my heart.

I wrote it in my journal. I turned it over through the day. I chewed on it, at first rejecting the implications, then welcoming them. This thought called up others from Scripture.

In his first letter, Peter exhorts persecuted first-century Christians to see themselves as separated from their world and set apart to God. He calls them "God's elect strangers"— or aliens—in the greeting of his letter. Then he tells them that their surest defense against their enemies will come through an understanding of their separated identity.

> Therefore, prepare your minds for action; be self-controlled; set your hope fully on the grace to be given you when Jesus Christ is revealed. As obedient children, do not conform to the evil desires you had when you lived in ignorance. But just as He who called you is holy, so be holy in all you do; for it is written: "Be holy, because I am holy" (1 Peter 1:13-16).

The word *holy* actually means "set apart." Those who are holy are God's set-apart saints.

"Separate thyself unto me." I made a decision to put on

emotional blinders to marriage. I pictured eighteenth-century horsedrawn London cabs. To prevent shying, a cabdriver fastened leather or metal blinders on the bridle of his horse so that it could see straight ahead without distraction.

I put on my blinders and covenanted with God that if He had marriage in my future, He would have to jerk my head around to notice a man. I was going ahead with Him. I was separating myself to Him and His purposes for my life. Single-mindedly, I was going to pursue intimacy with Him.

Eventually, He did jerk my head around, and my heart as well. I met and married a man perfectly fitted for me. But the conclusion God brought me to in my single days applies well to others waiting for the altar. When we walk the road of life alone, we do best if we face straight ahead, with blinders to all the distractions. Instead of clinging stubbornly to what we can't make happen, we can move forward to possess the goal of knowing God better, and of accomplishing what is possible.

To separate the self means to choose to live primarily in the direction of God. It means to select Him as a first priority and to order the rest of life around knowing Him.

In the Book of Proverbs, Solomon zeroes in on this selection of life directions. In chapter 1, he states his purpose: to instruct the young in knowledge, and discretion, and in wisdom (1:1-7). For the next eight chapters he contrasts the way of wisdom with the way of folly, casting Folly in the role of the evil prostitute and Wisdom as a woman of virtue. Through this literary device, Solomon exhorts his young readers to separate themselves unto only one mistress, Wisdom. In Solomon's day, young men faced temptations on two main fronts. The first was exploitation; the second, adultery, or selling their hearts to other gods. Chapter 7 describes Lady Folly beckoning to young men journeying down the road to wisdom.

> At the window of my house I looked out through the lattice.
> I saw among the simple, I noticed among the young men,

a youth who lacked judgment.
He was going down the street near her corner,
walking along in the direction of her house at twilight,
as the day was fading, as the dark of night set in.

Then out came a woman to meet him,
dressed like a prostitute and with crafty intent.
(She is loud and defiant, her feet never stay at home;
now in the street, now in the squares,
at every corner she lurks.) She took hold of him
and kissed him and with a brazen face she said:

"I have peace offerings at home;
today I fulfilled my vows. So I came out to meet you;
I looked for you and have found you!
I have covered my bed with colored linens from Egypt.
I have perfumed my bed with myrrh, aloes and
cinnamon.
Come, let's drink deep of love till morning;
let's enjoy ourselves with love! My husband is not at
home;
he has gone on a long journey.
He took his purse filled with money
and will not be home till full moon."

With persuasive words she led him astray;
she seduced him with her smooth talk
(Proverbs 7:6-21).

How familiar is that call! We hear Lady Folly beckoning us
to her doors to enjoy the fruits of the forbidden. "Why wait?"
she questions. "I have all you want right here: sex, intimacy, a
sense of belonging. You can have it now. Come and enjoy!"

It's as if she prepared her feast for us and us alone. As if
she were waiting all day for us to happen by. Telling us that
her husband is gone, she drags our hearts from God, while
reassuring us that He won't mind—He won't even know.

And in the darkness, when no one suspects, our hearts linger in her presence. Just a little taste, we rationalize. Only for a while, we bargain. We've waited so long to be wanted. So long.

> All at once he followed her
> like an ox going to the slaughter,
> like a deer stepping into a noose
> till an arrow pierces his liver,
> like a bird darting into a snare,
> little knowing it will cost him his life
> (Proverbs 7:22-23).

But what we think we want, we don't really. What we think will meet our needs and add meaning to our days is actually very deadly. For as we share our hearts with an idol, we dilute our love for God and twist our perception of His love for us.

God calls single people to a life that is separated unto Him. He calls us away from the temptations of exploitations and adultery, from the pursuit of the easy but forbidden fruit. He calls us to a life that is set apart.

SINGULARLY SINGLE

I see six characteristics, six actions, which separate single people unto God.

■ Take your life off "hold".

She raised the heavy cherrywood lid. Gingerly, she pulled back tissue and felt the smooth coolness of a china dinner plate. She lifted it to the light and enjoyed its transparency. Her eye caught the vanilla glow of her mother's wedding veil. Moving a handmade quilt, she located a sterling water pitcher which had been her grandmother's and found her face staring back from its shiny surface. She was thirty-three and single.

The hope chest symbolized so much of what she wished her life would be. Old-fashioned elegance filled with frilly but sturdy promises—promises which had never been kept. Carefully, she replaced the contents, item by item. In went the ivory fan her father had given her mother on their wedding day. In went the tea service she'd fallen in love with almost a decade ago. In went the dinner plate, never once honored with the love of a home-cooked meal. Unused except in dreams, her treasures vanished from sight as she dropped the heavy lid. She turned away, leaving her life buried in the bottom of a hope chest.

She's like so many of us who wait. We mortgage our present while dreaming of the future. We stop living now, waiting for a wedding day which may or may not come.

It is true that marriage helps to make life meaningful. It satisfies a need for companionship and provides purpose. It sharpens our strengths and reveals our weaknesses. But marriage isn't necessary for fulfillment. Having a spouse in a house doesn't make it a home.

Luci Swindoll has always been single. In her book *Wide My World, Narrow My Bed,* Luci shares her secret for filling her own life and the lives of others with meaning.

Don't wait for a mate. Don't wait for more time.
Don't wait until both your feet are on the ground.
Don't wait for *anything else.*
The time to be involved with living is now—
not tomorrow or next week or next year. Now.

You say, "There are so many problems with being single.
I'm lonely, I'm bored, I don't know how to enjoy things
by myself." Of course there are problems.
There are problems in any lifestyle,
because that is a part of the living process. . . .

I would venture to say many of your problems
as a single person exist because you are holding back.
You're waiting for something better to come along,
that certain something that will enrich your circumstances.
Well, Friends,—it's here. It's called Life.
And Breath. And God. That's all you need.

You don't have to be married to be happy.
You just have to be alive.[5]

Henry David Thoreau wrote, "The man who goes alone can start today; but he who travels with another must wait until the other is ready." Take your life off hold! Open up that hope chest. Pull out the dishes, the silver pitcher and the tea set and put them to good use with some old-fashioned hospitality. Dig your life out of the hopes for tomorrow and invest it in the realities of today. Stop waiting and start living!

■ Make God your mate.

If you're single, there's one thing you hate to receive in the mail: a wedding invitation. Weddings remind singles of what they don't have.

In his book *Reaching Out,* Henri Nouwen writes of the ups and downs of solitude.

To wait for moments or places where no pain exists, no separation is felt, and where all human restlessness has turned into inner peace is waiting for a dreamworld. No friend or lover, no husband or wife, no community or commune will be able to put to rest our deepest cravings for unity and wholeness.[6]

Only God can fill our deepest void. And only in loving Him are we able to love others.

There's a sense in which marriage to God is the best practice for marriage to a mortal. When we enter into an intimate relationship with God, we wed ourselves to trust, honor and obey, to love, cherish and uphold, to forsake all others and to keep ourselves only unto Him. In such a relationship, we learn the intimacy, devotion, and self-sacrifice necessary to make a marriage between mortals work, while meeting our very mortal needs at the same time.

Long before and even after entering into marriage, make God your first mate. Learn from Him how to meet the needs of another and how to have your needs met in Him alone.

■ Prepare for battle.

Those who are single will encounter battlegrounds uniquely fitted to their circumstances. Consider the following battlefields.

It's Saturday night and your roommate has a date, just like every other Saturday night. You don't, just like every other Saturday night. While roomie has a good time, resentment accompanies you through the evening and long into the lonely night.

As you dress in the morning, insecurity whispers messages of inadequacy in your ear. If you had a better job . . . if you had a more developed body . . . if you had more money and could buy the right clothes . . . if you weren't so shy. Lies attack your self-image, threatening its very foundation.

A coworker notices you. Eureka! After coffee breaks, luncheons, and casual phone conversations, you go out on a date. As you say good-night, you touch, you linger, you weaken. Impulses dart from your skin to your stomach to your toes when, tenderly kissed, you're nudged into your apartment. You know you're faced with a choice. What will it really matter? You long to be wanted the way you're wanted now.

"Separate thyself unto Me." Through the battlegrounds of resentment, of erroneous self-talk, of quick and easy intimacy, comes the call of God. He doesn't call us to a set-apart singleness because He wants to deprive, punish, or control. He calls us to a set-apart singleness for the same reason He calls us to a set-apart holiness in whatever state we are in. In all of life, whether single or married, God desires that His people demonstrate to His world that they first belong to Him.

■ Create a family.

Every human being needs the security that parents, mates, siblings and children provide. God made us that way, and He incorporated measures to meet such needs when He designed the family: the church. Within its walls we can find spiritual moms and dads, adopt spiritual sons and daughters, relate to one another as brother and sister—all while we allow God to father and husband us.

The most completely single person who ever walked the earth knew His needs well enough to create a family for Himself. He chose twelve to be spiritual companions and related to them as brothers. He welcomed women as His sisters. He cherished His mother, Mary, and from the cross provided for her future by asking John to "adopt" her as his own mother. Though He was single, Jesus was a family man.

In a different way, so was Paul. While we know little of his physical family, the Bible makes plain that Paul created a family for himself from the Christian community. Barnabas big-brothered him, pushing a path through the skepticism of the disciples so that Paul might gain a hearing. Timothy served him as a son, learning practical Christianity from Paul's example. Priscilla and Aquila, co-laborers in the Gospel, shared his life as siblings.

If you have few natural loved ones, you can create a family for yourself from your community. Look about your life for spiritual relatives. Who sweated and strained as you were born into the faith? Reach out to your spiritual parents and repay the gift of life they gave you in Christ. In their old age, or their time of need, reciprocate.

Who shares your vision, your heart, your commitment to Christ? Welcome that individual as a brother or sister. Elbow to elbow, accompany each other through life's challenges.

Who needs the guidance, protection and love of a parent? While you may never have a natural child, there's a passel of orphans out there waiting to be spiritually adopted into the family of God. Speaking of the future glory of Zion, Isaiah writes beautiful words about the barren turned fruitful. His meaning can apply to the single who produces spiritual children for the kingdom of God.

> "Sing, O barren woman, you who never bore a child; burst into song, shout for joy, you who were never in labor; because more are the children of the desolate woman than of her who has a husband," says the Lord (Isaiah 54:1).

51

Singles need not be alone. Look around your world for would-be relatives. If there are no natural ties to bind, blessed be the spiritual!

■ Give God space to work.

Tear up your checklist. Let go of your expectations. Yield yourself to your wait. Most people will marry . . . eventually. As you set yourself apart to God, give Him space to work out His will in your particular set of circumstances.

God needs space to work in two areas. The first is on *who we are*. Harold Ivan Smith writes,

> Singleness is more than a hunting season. It is a time to grow, to stretch, to conquer, and to learn. Some of us are not ready for marriage because we have not learned the essentials. We have not mastered those resources which are vital to the survival and growth of a marriage.[7]

As a person in waiting, give God the space He needs to work. Maybe you need to lose some extra pounds. Work on your wardrobe. Develop a sense of personal style. Define your person with individualized hobbies and pastimes. Get a handle on your areas of weakness.

God has preparation work to do in us to make us ready for marriage and whatever else lies ahead of us. When we back off, we give Him the space He needs to accomplish His good pleasure—and ours. Let the Creator of your being hone you into a unique and special somebody.

In his devotional classic *Waiting on God!* Andrew Murray mirrors this thought: "We must not only think of our waiting upon God, but also of what is more wonderful still, of God's waiting upon us."[8]

Second, God needs space to work on *what we want*. Connell O'Brien Cowan and Melvyn Kinder, in their book *Smart Women, Foolish Choices,* suggest that many women stay single because they have unhealthy expectations for "Mr. Right."

There are a lot of men who may not fit the mold that

many women have in mind when they think of "Mr. Right" . . . men who may have visible flaws in behavior or appearance; men who may be initially insecure when it comes to forming relationships. They may not have the "look"; they may be awkward conversationalists. Worst of all, they may be too available, too eager. But they are often men who possess great possibilities. They truly are "diamonds in the rough". . . .

There are a great many men—and, of course, women—who are very slow in revealing themselves. They are usually people who have experienced rejection in some form in the past and, having been once burned, are now "twice shy." The smart woman should know how to get past this exterior awkwardness that many men may display.[9]

We may think we know what we want, but do we? It's better to be single than to be married to the wrong person. Whether in relationships, careers, or callings, God may need to work on what we want in order to fit us with what we need.

■ Develop a good memory.

While every married person was once single, few remember what it's like to be single. They invite singles to dinner only when a date is provided, forgetting that they hated the habitual "pairing up" of their unmarried days. They forget to include a single in an activity of mostly couples, believing that the unmarried person would be uneasy; they overlook the greater pain of being uninvited. They also dump extra duties on single churchgoers, assuming that they have more time, and ignore a single's added responsibilities in a home where there is no one to share the workload or contribute a paycheck.

The engaged can also become forgetful of the single dilemma. Listening for their own wedding bells, they are eager to toss aside the struggles of singlehood for those of marital bliss and become absentminded about their peers.

Set-apart singles will develop good memories about their single days. Unlike the Israelites in the wilderness who forgot about the pillar of fire and the manna from heaven the moment their feet touched the Promised Land, singles who want their days alone to count will remember the experience even when it is over. When God does work in a life, He does not want it to be forgotten.

THE PERMANENT STATE OF SEPARATENESS

You who wait for mates, wait at the right gate; sit on the steps of Lady Wisdom and avoid the beckoning call of Lady Folly. Separate yourself unto God.

Then, wait in the right way. Take your life off hold, make God your mate, prepare for battle on the obvious fronts of attack, create a family for yourself, give God space to work and develop a good memory about these days of waiting.

Separate yourself unto God. Singleness is not necessarily a calling for a lifetime. But separation is a calling to a life that will endure for all time. If your wait for a mate comes to an end, don't abandon your calling to a singled-out, separated life when you stand at the altar. Frame it as a credo above the mantle of a marriage where two become one, singled out and separated unto God. And if your wait for a mate never ceases, may you be found waiting like the virgin for the bridegroom, her lamp trimmed and her heart tidied, truly ready to receive Him at last.

5

WAITING
for a Child

The most ironic of human conditions is infertility, where millions of miracle-seekers are trying desperately to accomplish what most of the world is trying desperately to avoid.[1]

Fallow, noun: cultivated land allowed to lie idle during the growing season. Fallow, verb: to plow, harrow and break up land without seeding. Fallow, adjective: left untilled or unsown after plowing. Dormant. Inactive. Infertile.

When our plans for parenthood are thwarted, we find our lives fallow. Oh, how it hurts! The soil of our marriage has been plowed and harrowed but no seed has been planted. Like clods of dirt, turned and tilled, we await our chance to bear life, to offer up the sacrifice of reproduction, to participate in the miracle of birth.

And yet nothing grows. We wait, while the spring edges into summer. We wait, feeling the chill of autumn's approach. We wait. And the only crop that grows in the soil of our lives is the root of bitter disappointment.

Infertility is defined as "the inability to conceive after a year of unprotected regular intercourse, or the inability to carry a pregnancy to a live birth."[2] Thus, the category includes those

55

who are childless because they cannot conceive, as well as those who conceive but are unable to carry a child to term—everything from sterility to miscarriage to stillbirth.

Others, not technically considered infertile, share the waiting experience of the fallow field. These are the single individuals who desire to parent but remain celibate, the couple carrying genetic diseases, as well as parents who have lost a child to death after birth and are unable to have another.

Among the childless couples of our country, infertility is cited as the most common reason for their fallow condition. Almost twenty percent of all American couples who try to have children encounter difficulties.[3] Of those who do conceive, fifteen to twenty percent will lose their child before the end of the twentieth week of the pregnancy. In fact, more lives are lost in the first twenty weeks than in any other period of pregnancy.[4]

Fallow fields. Empty earth. The barren are those who wait for the gift of giving forth life.

THE BURDEN OF BARRENNESS

Infertility has been called "the quiet crisis." Lynda Rutledge Stephenson, author of *Give Us a Child*, suggests that *crises* may be a better word.

It begins as a medical crisis. This leads to a social crisis that comes with the peer pressure to have children. Sometimes an ethical crisis results from new medical technologies, such as artificial insemination and surrogate mothering. Ultimately, the situation may lead to a spiritual crisis.[5]

Adjustment to such a series of crises is a heavy matter. Five burdens add weight to the barren.

■ The emotional burden: Roller-coaster reactions.
A support group for infertiles published the following column in their newsletter.

You know it's going to be a bad day when ...

–Your infertility specialist posts the following sign in his office: "We only accept cash for visits and tests. Please pay before leaving."

–Your new puppy chews up three months worth of basal temperature charts.

–The country where you're adopting a baby has a major military coup and all travel in and out of the country grinds to a halt.

–The only seat on the bus is beside a very pregnant woman with a cute two-year-old squirming on what's left of her lap.

–Your Clomid prescription comes in a child-proof cap.

–You see a *60 Minutes* film crew and Dan Rather entering your adoption agency.

–Your houseguests mistake the twenty-four-hour urine collection in the refrigerator for cider.[6]

The trauma of waiting for a child roller-coasters your emotions. One minute you're up and convinced that this time you're pregnant. The next second you're plunged into despair, furious at the cruel joke your body has played on you.

You feel like you're stuck in limbo. The "baby quest" occupies all your thoughts, prayers, and dreams. You plan your existence around the hoped-for state of parenthood. I know of one woman who lives in a building with an elevator so she won't have to exert herself on stairs if she gets pregnant. Another works only at part-time jobs so she won't have to disappoint an employer.

I have a friend who theorizes that it's easier to plan around pregnancy than infertility. Her views are echoed by another would-be parent who says,

Infertiles are like those hamsters who play for hours on a wheel, going nowhere, never getting off. Around you life spins by—your career, your family, your marriage, your friends—without your participation. Useless motion consumes you, while the faintest glimmer of hope prevents you from moving on with life.[7]

Besides feeling stuck in limbo, a woman is haunted by threats of inadequacy. Ann Kiemel Anderson reports a great sense of failure and worthlessness following a series of miscarriages. Messages of failure bombard the couple, pelting down insecurity. She wonders, "How can I be a woman and not be able to mother?" He questions, "What kind of man am I?"

Further, you wonder if you're really a grown-up as you struggle with feelings of immaturity. Barbara Eck Menning, founder of a national infertility support organization called RESOLVE, comments that because parenting is often a major life goal, when it is blocked for a long period of time, serious developmental crises can result. You feel stunted in your maturity, an adolescent for life.

Between these valleys of limbo, inadequacy, and immaturity are the highs of hope which come with a delayed menstrual cycle and the peaks of independence when you take off to Hawaii while your friends are saddled with squawking babies. Up and down, up and back down again, the roller-coaster reactions of barrenness. It's enough to make you sick.

■ The physical burden: Body betrayal.

The physical burden of infertility is enormous. Suddenly your body, which has been like a loyal friend, mutinies. You feel betrayed when it won't cooperate. "No one warned me that in waiting for the ideal moment to become a parent, one might lose that moment altogether," comments one with a rebel body.[8]

Part of the physical burden is the humiliation of the infertility workup. Sperm counts, postcoital tests, artificial insemination—the sacred act of conception goes on display before the critical eyes of the medical community. Even with the most empathetic specialists, the infertile couple experiences a sense of invasion.

Such inspection of your sexual organs and their functions impacts your sexual relationship. Sex becomes a chore rather than an expression of love. Spontaneity is gone. When the right hour of the right day arrives—presto! you must make love or forget your chances of pregnancy for another month. Unfortunately, temperature charts and desires don't always match up. Sex becomes a homework assignment, done on time, and handed in to be graded by the doctor.

■ The relational burden: Marriage equals parenthood. Psychologists point out that infertility makes couples take a harder look at each other at a time when most other married folks are focused only on taking care of children.[9] Looking so intently within the marriage unit brings about two problems.

First, it's easy to start blaming. Whose fault is it that we can't have a baby? Whether silent or spoken, this question whispers through the thinking of wedded unparents.

In the old days, everyone blamed infertility on the woman. As recently as 1960, it was believed that women accounted for ninety percent of barrenness. If a man could have an erection and produce some sperm, he was assumed to be fertile.[10] Today medical experts hold that infertility problems are about forty percent due to female irregularities and forty percent due to male. In the remaining cases, both partners have some responsibility.[11]

The question of who is to blame rattles around in a marriage until the couple is so desperate for children that they risk finding out. Once the evidence is in, if it can in fact be gathered, partners arm-wrestle anxiety. The fertile partner, in fits of disloyal despair, struggles with unmentionable wonderings like, "What if I'd married someone else?" The infertile mate pauses over previously ridiculous thoughts like, "What if my love goes elsewhere to parent? What if I lose my partner to infidelity?"

■ The social burden: Baby bloopers. The marital relationship isn't all that suffers in the crises of barrenness. Relatives can get in the way of those who are not in a "family way." Parents, eager to be grandparents, may invade your despair while hunting for clues as to when you're going to "get serious and settle down." Siblings may hatch out their young at a pace comparable to the Old Woman who lived in a shoe, rekindling old rivalries. Even in the church family, young marrieds' classes burst at the seams with babies, and social gatherings seem to center around the details of birth and child development.

Holidays and special occasions are treacherous. Participation in any event where the presence or absence of children is obvious leaves you trampled by feelings of isolation, aloneness, and separation.

The well-meant remarks of those around add to this sense of isolation. "Take a vacation and relax!" you hear, after you just returned from Mexico. "Oh, you ought to adopt! My friends got pregnant two months after they adopted a little boy. Now they have four!" "You ought to appreciate the free time you have." "What a joy it must be not to have to use birth control!" Gag!

Columnist Erma Bombeck, who was childless for the first six years of her marriage and then suffered two miscarriages, comments on the social burden of infertility: "[Infertile folks] get about as much sympathy as an eigthy-three-pound woman who is trying to gain weight." A husband in an infertile couple said, "Every time our friends conceived, we died a little."

■ The spiritual burden: The curse of empty quivers. When you turn to the Bible, you may feel that instead of receiving comfort in its pages, you are among the cursed. Instructing Israel about keeping the Law, Moses wrote,

> He will love you and bless you and increase your numbers. He will bless the fruit of your womb, the crops of your land—your grain, new wine and oil—the calves of your herds and the lambs of your flocks in the land that He swore to your forefathers to give you. You will be blessed more than any other people; none of your men or women will be childless, nor any of your livestock without young (Deuteronomy 7:13-14).

The obvious conclusion was that when Israel obeyed God,

God blessed Israel with children. When Israel disobeyed, God withheld young. How about these verses from the Psalms?

> He raises the poor from the dust
> and lifts the needy from the ash heap.
> He seats them with princes,
> with the princes of their people.
> He settles the barren woman in her home
> as a happy mother of children. Praise the Lord
> (Psalm 113:7-9).

> Sons are a heritage from the Lord,
> children a reward from Him.
> Like arrows in the hands of a warrior
> are sons born in one's youth.
> Blessed is the man whose quiver is full of them
> (Psalm 127:3-5).

What's a Christian couple to do with such verses? Are children indeed a symbol of God's great pleasure with our obedience and the lack of them a curse?

A look at the lives of the infertile couples in Scripture indicates otherwise. Five couples wept through their waits for children. In no case was a couple denied children because of disobedience. Sarah and Abraham, Rebekah and Isaac, Rachel and Jacob, Hannah and Elkanah, Elizabeth and Zechariah—all these couples waited for a child, wondering if God were disappointed in them or absent from their lives.

We see instances where God had compassion on the unloved and gave children as a means of comfort as He did to Leah, who was loved less than her sister, Rachel, by their husband Jacob. We see occasions of disobedience as in the case of Sarah and Abraham, where Abraham once passed Sarah off as his sister, and where Sarah gave Abraham her maidservant so they might have a son. But their barrenness is not attributed to these acts. In the case of Elizabeth and Zechariah, we're told, "Both of them were upright in the sight of God, observing all the Lord's commandments and regulations blame-lessly. But they had no children" (Luke 1:6-7).

One of the greatest burdens on those waiting for a child is the sense that God is somehow punishing, judging, or with-holding a blessing because of disobedience. You muse over past indiscretions, and guilt assaults your conscience. Confu-sion over what it takes to please God mounts in your heart. Fear over messing up again looms, forecasting future failures.

Even when the weight is cast aside long enough to "run the race," as the author of Hebrews encourages us to do, you're torn between running for your goal or your God. You want God, but you equally long for the fulfillment of your desires. Ann Kiemel Anderson writes, "How human it is to want God, but not God exclusively. We long for God *with* all the externals added on."[12]

The barren struggle under the load of emotional, physical, relational, social and spiritual burdens.

WAITING CRADLES

Because of a physical problem resulting from an illness, my husband, Evan, and I knew when we married that we could not have children. From the altar on, we planned to adopt. We got married, honeymooned in Mexico, unpacked our worldly possessions in a condo and applied to an adoption agency. Since we had a substantial wait ahead of us, it helped that neither of us was in a hurry to become a parent. Evan contin-ued to build a career in business. I finished up seminary and plunged into my work as dean of women at a Bible college. I loved my three-pronged responsibilities of counseling, teach-ing, and administrating.

During my third year at the college, the adoption agency informed us that we'd moved off the "inactive" list. This meant it was time for our "home study," an indepth series of inter-views and psychological probings through which the agency would determine our suitability for parenthood. We were ap-proved in December of that year and the agency guaranteed a baby by the next December. I resigned my position in May and went home to wait.

In June I wallpapered the nursery walls and painted a chest of drawers. I embroidered a quilt and a matching sheet and pillow set. In July I was asked to try my hand at a radio program on behalf of the college where I had been employed. Because I was waiting, I agreed.

In the fall I closed the nursery door, threw myself into the radio scripts, avoided baby showers, and envied my pregnant friends. I picked dates for receiving a baby at random and prayed madly toward them. They passed without event.

My anguish erupted in the ears of my husband and my best friend. But God got the worst of it. I was furious with Him. I was frustrated, depressed and sick of being on hold! I'd left my job, my ministry, and all that had filled my life with meaning. Was God going to leave me on the shelf forever? Surely, He'd forgotten my need. He'd overlooked my situation. Had He meant to string me along all this time? When could I get on with what I was supposed to do, with what mattered?

When Thanksgiving came, I was convinced that we'd receive a baby by Christmas. After all, the agency had promised. It became my bottom-line prayer. We set up a special Christmas tree, tied the branches with pink-and-blue satin ribbons, stuffed it full of baby's breath and christened it our "hope-for-the-baby" tree. Each morning I knelt beneath it and poured out my heart's desire to God. "A baby by Christmas, please God, please."

On December 21 the phone rang. It was another waiting mother from our home study group. She and her husband were the only couple besides Evan and me who had not received a promised baby during the past year. Over the past months we'd chatted on the phone, sharing our impatience. This time she was not calling with tears of sadness but with tears of joy. They had a boy.

My best efforts produced only a lukewarm, "Congratulations, I'm so happy for you." I hung up and called our social worker and asked her to be blunt. Was there any hope that we'd receive a baby by Christmas? She was blunt. No, there was no hope.

The phone hit the cradle with a crack. I felt as though I'd been shot. The air left my chest. I crumpled to the floor. From somewhere deep within the caverns of my heart came the cry of a wounded animal. It must have been ten minutes before I could move. I found myself in front of the "hope-for-the-baby" tree, and staring at its twinkling symbol of hope, I started sobbing.

After a Christmas of brave smiles and forced laughter, we decided to leave the "hope-for-the-baby" tree up until we received a baby, but took it down in February because it seemed a little silly. I'd come to the place where I kept praying out of sheer obedience, but it was hard to believe it would help.

Over the next few months, life's pace quickened. Ministry came off the shelf and into focus clearer than ever before. The radio program I'd been writing and hosting was picked up by Denver Seminary and was syndicated nationally. Every so often I'd peek in the nursery and wonder, "Is it ever to be a part of our lives?" I'd open the drawers and touch the bonnets, booties, and bedding that were for our baby. I'd run my hands over the threads of my crude embroidery. Would there ever be curious little fingers to pull at those stitches? Had God forgotten? Had He misplaced my order?

During this time, I made a friend. Perhaps it was because she too waited for a child that we grew so close during those years. Her words expressed my feelings. Her honesty about her pain taught me to be honest about mine. Her determination to stay near God motivated me to remember Him, even when I thought He'd forgotten me.

■ A case study of an Infertile Myrtle.

You've heard of Fertile Myrtles. They're women who, after a disaster, could repopulate the earth in their lifetime. Even when they wish they could stop having babies, they can't.

This woman was an Infertile Myrtle, though most people knew her simply as Hannah. She was the wife a man named Elkanah, who was also married to a woman named Peninnah.

Peninnah had children but Hannah had none. That's the complete description of Hannah's character. She had no children.

For years Elkanah took his family to the central sanctuary at Shiloh to make sacrifices to God. There were three specific occasions where men were required to present offerings. Most likely the festival described in 1 Samuel 1 is the Feast of Tabernacles, when Israel commemorated God's care for people during their journey to Canaan and His blessing on the year's crops.

"Thankfulness for the year's crops? How about the lack of them?" Hannah must have thought. She was but a fallow field, next to a very fertile one. Here was Peninnah, the wife her husband had taken to give him sons because Hannah couldn't produce, the perennial Fertile Myrtle—with a belly swollen with child, thanking God for His great blessings.

And how she thanked God! "O Lord! Thank You for Your kind hand of blessing! You have said that children are a reward from You! They are a heritage! Through Your great gift of children, You have given woman a purpose for existence!" Then a sidelong glance at Hannah and when she was sure Hannah had heard, "Oh, to serve You with our fruitful wombs! Oh, to yield to You great crops for Your kingdom! Indeed, blessed is the woman You have settled in a home as a happy mother of children!" Then with smug self-importance, she waddled her weight toward a chair, watching Hannah wince under the burden of her barrenness. What offering could this fallow field bring to God?

As I read of Hannah's plight at the Feast of Tabernacles, I thought of my own struggle with Mother's Day, when our church was filled with corsaged mothers honored as privileged life-givers and shapers. Year after year I watched the Fertile Myrtles and waited for my turn.

And Hannah? She obediently attended each Feast Day, wondering how she could thank God for producing a bountiful crop in others while leaving her field fallow. Year after year.

But one year, when the ceremony and celebrating had ended, Hannah rose and, "in bitterness of soul," wept and prayed to God. "In bitterness of soul" is the phrase used of Job six times as he begged God for wisdom during his torturous trials. In bitterness of soul, Hannah reached out to the God she felt had forgotten her and made a vow.

> O Lord Almighty, if You will only look
> upon Your servant's misery and remember me,
> and not forget Your servant but give her a son,
> then I will give him to the Lord
> for all the days of his life,
> and no razor will ever be used on his head
> (1 Samuel 1:11).

Numbers 30 describes the conditions whereby a woman's vow was to be upheld. If she was married and her husband objected to her vow, he could renege on it. If her husband made no objection, then he was obligated to it just as if he'd made it himself. Hannah made reference to the Nazarite vow when she promised not to cut her boy's hair. But where most Nazarite vows were made as a symbol of service for a designated period of time, Hannah vowed for a lifetime. This kind of dedication was a complete and irrevocable giving up of a child to God.

Hannah's vow was no small matter. She wasn't offering lip service to God. When Eli, the priest, observed Hannah in deep prayer, he accused her of being drunk. But Hannah's vow was not an emotional surge from too many glasses of bubbly. She responded to Eli,

> Not so, my lord . . . I am a woman who is deeply
> troubled. I have not been drinking wine or beer;
> I was pouring out my soul to the Lord.
> Do not take your servant for a wicked woman;
> I have been praying here out of my great anguish and
> grief (1 Samuel 1:15-16).

As if reading back over the spiritual diary of her life, Hannah recalled who God was. And remembering the very Person of Yahweh, the Lord Almighty, she asked that He would also remember her.

In Hebrew, the word *remember* is more than simple recall. The word is used in Genesis 8:1, when Noah had been in the ark for 150 days without hearing from God. During that long period of silence Noah might have wondered when, or if, the ark would land. "God remembered Noah and all the wild animals and the livestock that were with him in the ark, and he sent a wind over the earth, and the waters receded." When Hannah asked that God remember her, she was requesting that He go into action on her behalf.

As Eli heard the earnestness of Hannah's prayer, he responded, "Go in peace, and may the God of Israel grant you what you have asked of Him" (1:17). Hannah and Elkanah returned to their home in Ramah and "Elkanah lay with Hannah his wife, and the Lord remembered her" (1:19).

Hannah remembered God and God remembered Hannah. Hannah again remembered God as she named her son *Samuel,* meaning "heard of God" or "asked of God." And when he was about three years old and weaned, she and Elkanah fulfilled the vow they had made by taking him to Shiloh and giving him back to God for lifetime service. Hannah said to Eli,

> I prayed for this child,
> and the Lord has granted me what I asked of Him.
> So now I give him to the Lord.
> For his whole life he will be given over to the Lord
> (1 Samuel 1:27-28).

She left her firstborn and returned to life with Elkanah and Peninnah, no longer fallow but fertile. Hannah had five other children, three sons and two daughters. Her son Samuel grew to be the prophet through whom God anointed the first and second kings of Israel.

■ God's good memory.

My husband and I had waited for almost four and one-half

years. The radio ministry was flourishing, and in its growth, the bitterness of my heart was easing.

It was an April day, the Saturday before Easter. I'd planned a shower for an engaged friend and woke up that morning to a blizzard. I spent most of the morning on the phone postponing the party, while Evan took off with a friend in a four-wheel-drive to play racquetball.

I curled up in a chair in the family room, pulled out a yellow pad and started jotting down what I remembered over the past year about the waiting process. Through the "bitterness of soul" of my long wait, God had given me a ministry in radio. If my life had not been placed on hold, the seed of that ministry would never have been planted. I would have been too busy with mothering to allow myself to consider it.

Just then the phone rang. I padded over to answer it and stood numb as I listened to the voice of our social worker. We had a baby girl!

Because the next day was Easter Sunday, we were to pick Eva up on Monday. On Easter morning, Evan and I stood in the worship service, eyes glued to a rough cross that had been erected on the platform, and sang, "Jesus Christ is risen to-day! Alleluia!" Tears trickled down our faces. The long wait was almost over. God had remembered—and we would never forget. With Hannah, we rejoiced, "For this child we prayed and the Lord has granted what we asked of Him."

We have a daughter and now a son, also through adoption. No two waits are alike. Where we waited four and one-half years for Eva, we waited a relatively short two and one-half years for Ethan.

The reality of infertility continues even after the quiver has been filled. As one writer puts it, "Adoption is a way of having a family, not a Tylenol for the grief of infertility."[13] Barbara Eck Menning, the founder of RESOLVE comments,

My infertility resides in my heart like an old friend.
I do not hear from it for weeks at a time,
and then, a moment, a thought, a baby announcement

68

or some such thing, and I will feel the tug—
maybe even be sad or shed a few tears.
And I think, "There's my old friend,"
It will always be part of me. . . . [14]

God's promise to Hannah is His promise to me and to you. God does not forget those who remember Him.

Many fallow fields will one day become fertile. Infertility experts report that pregnancy is a goal achievable by seventy percent of infertile couples, and that parenting is a life role objective possible for many more through alternative ways.[15]

Others will remain fallow, in terms of childbearing. But even those fields can become fruitful for God as they offer up their ground to God.

In Isaiah 53:8, the Suffering Servant is said to have no descendants, a considerable tragedy in the Old Testament. But in this prophetic chapter, the writer promises that the Messiah will have many spiritual offspring (Isaiah 53:10).

He, who is responsible for all growth in our lives, can harvest a spiritual fruit of righteousness out of unproductive and unpromising soil. He can make the fallow life fruitful through the sharing of our gifts with His church and also with those who don't yet know Him as Lord.

In some way, God will come to make the fallow fruitful. God will not forget those who remember Him.

6
WAITING
for the Fish to Bite

The first time I went fishing, I was a novice of twenty-three years, outfitted with a rod, a boat, and a guide to bait my hook and tell me where to cast it. Gliding down the North Platte River in Wyoming, I plunked a loaded hook into a smooth pool and pulled out a foot-long rainbow trout. Squealing with delight, I maneuvered him to the guide who removed my catch and stuffed him into a basket, whereupon he baited me up and pointed me to another pool to repeat my success.

In an hour and a half, I'd graduated from amateur to expert. I never touched a worm or the slimy skin of a fish. I never struggled with a tangled line. And I never, never, never waited for the fish to bite. This was fishing!

Six years later I returned to the same spot and floated along in a similar boat, holding a similar rod, baited by a similar guide. I dropped hook after hook into the pools he pinpointed. And time after time, I reeled in empty lines. There was nothing wrong with the bait. This guide was as expert as the first one. The river had been stocked as before. My efforts were as sincere. But I caught nothing. The fish just weren't biting.

After swapping fish stories with others, I've concluded that my second adventure in fishing is more the norm and my first

71

the exception. More often than not, between casting and catching comes a period of waiting.

WHEN THE FISH WON'T BITE

The Bible clearly directs us to go into all the world and make disciples. We take such a command seriously, because knowing God has made a difference in our days and we're anxious to share this life-changing knowledge with others, especially those we love. We want our parents, our children, our husband or wife, and our friends to have what we have. We don't want to go to heaven without them.

Because we take God seriously, both in what He's done in us and in what He wants to do, it's tough when the people we love don't respond to the God we love. When we bait up a hook, cast it in a promising pool and pull it back empty, we wonder what went wrong.

■ In the hollow of our hearts we vacillate.
After telling a friend about the best Friend we've ever had, we expect a reaction. How could something so important to us be so unimportant to him? Our emotions swing back and forth. First, we feel guilty. We wonder what we did wrong in presenting the Gospel. Did we come on too heavy? Should we have pushed harder for a decision? Were we clear? Were we boring?

Next we wonder what in our lives keeps others from God? Are we too spiritual? Are we too vulnerable about the doubts we still have? Are we too sinful to be used by God?

When loved ones we know don't trust Christ, we feel responsible. Guilt assaults us, accusing us of failing in our proclamation of the Gospel.

We also feel afraid. Our minds pencil the names of family members and friends on a mental checklist. Grandpa will be in heaven but Grandma won't. Little Jamie hasn't made a decision yet and he's headed out on an overnight field trip this weekend. A husband doesn't know God and lives as if he thinks he'll never die. But one day he will. What then?

72

■ Thinking with our hearts, we react.
And as guilt and fear dig into our thinking, we move into action. Sometimes we push harder. We pounce on wives, parents, children and coworkers with a message of repentance. We decorate our homes with religious mementos, counting on the conviction of their clichés. We manipulate spouses to attend Bible studies. We cajole teenagers into church. We barge into the privacy of a neighbor's life, nosing about for another chance to share the Gospel.

Other times we withdraw. Because we've told the story of Jesus once with no results, we assume we should never broach the subject again. We figure folks know what to do if they really want to. When the subject nears God, we change it. When someone sniffs out the importance of Jesus in our lives, we minimize it. With those who don't know God, we work to blend in with the landscape.

Both reactions are understandable. We feel guilty and we feel afraid. So we either go for the jugular or we go away.

A FISH STORY

While we're waiting for the fish to bite, we ponder the mysteries of evangelism. Who is responsible for what in evangelism? What part of bringing folks to Christ is God's job and what part is ours?

Luke 5 records how the first evangelists were called and what it was they were to do. In its telling, we gain an understanding of the roles of man and God in evangelism.

The incident occurred near the start of Jesus' ministry. Andrew, Peter's brother, had been a follower of John the Baptist. As such, he'd witnessed Jesus' baptism, and subsequently began to hang around Jesus. John 1:40-42 tells us that he found Peter (then called Simon) and took him back to Jesus. Evidently, the three, along with a few others, spent some time together because Jesus visited their home. Mark 1:29-31 reveals Jesus ministering to Peter's mother-in-law.

A while later, Jesus was looking for a platform from which

to teach and, spotting the brothers by their boats at the seashore, found it natural to enlist their aid. Luke 5:3 tells us that Jesus got into Peter's boat and asked him to cast out from shore just far enough to distance them from the crowd but so that He could still be heard. Then, from His floating pulpit, Jesus sat down and taught.

Luke doesn't record the subject of Jesus' message, but I can't help wondering whether His words were addressed to the crowd or to Peter. For it was just as He finished speaking that Jesus instructed Peter to venture into the deep water and let the nets down.

Now Peter knew that the best time for fishing had passed. He and Andrew had spent themselves during the prime hours of the night, without success. What were the chances of a catch at this time of day?

In addition, Peter knew that Jesus was directing them past the best place for fishing—fish gathered in shoals, or schools, in the shallower parts of the sea. Fishermen worked together, one watching for the movement of fish beneath the water and the other casting the net. In taking the boat into deeper waters, Jesus was directing them to go where they couldn't sight a catch. But Peter was struck by the authority of his passenger. In spite of his fishing expertise and regardless of his doubts, Peter responded, "Because You say so, I will let down the nets." Luke then tells us,

> When they had done so, they caught such a large number of fish that their nets began to break. So they signaled their partners in the other boat to come and help them, and they came and filled both boats so full that they began to sink (5:6-7).

In prime time and select spots they had caught nothing. But when Jesus commanded them to cast their nets—when He was present in the boat—the nets came up bursting with fish.

Such a moment wasn't wasted on Peter. He knew fish—their eating habits, their swimming routes, their daily cycles.

74

Summer, winter, spring, and fall, Peter fished. Good weather and bad, Peter fished. Well or worn out, Peter fished. He made his living on the sea, out of the very boat which was now sinking with its prodigious haul. Struggling to land the catch, eyes ogling the pile of flapping fins, heart stunned at the miracle of these events, Peter bowed before Jesus.

The night before, he had brought his training, his equipment, and his experience to the sea in search of fish. But for all his efforts, he had returned with an empty boat. Now the fish nose-dived for the nets. But had Peter not cast the nets, there would have been no catch. Likewise, if Jesus had not been in the boat, the fish would not have bitten.

"From now on," Jesus promised, "you will catch men." Then Peter, his brother Andrew, and his partners, James and John, left their boats, their nets, their bait, and their expertise in fishing for fish to follow after One who would teach them to fish for men.

■ Our responsibility: Go fishing.

We're just told to go fishing—we're not responsible for getting the fish to bite. Our responsibility as recipients of God's grace is to share the good news with others. The Bible says nothing about making them receive it. Nothing about forcing others to accept it. We just have to offer it, to share it, to tell it.

Michael Cocoris is a pastor in California who spent some fifteen years of his ministry traveling around the country as an evangelist. Preaching from this same text in Luke 5 he concludes,

Very simply put, the key to catching men is that you are obedient. That you simply take the command that God has given us that says we're to go into all the world and preach the Gospel to every creature and then you just go do it.

And you do it. And you do it some more. You do it in the winter and in the summer and in the spring and in the fall. You do it in the morning and in the evening. You do it when the sun is shining and when clouds give an overcast to the day. You do it when you're full of energy. You do it when you feel like it and you do it when you don't feel like it and you just do it. And you do it. And you do it. And you do it. And you do it. And you do it, do it, do it. The key to catching fish is that you go fishing.[1]

■ God's responsibility: Get the fish to bite.
It's up to us to fish. Day after day we are to offer the bait. God's job is to get the fish to bite. J.I. Packer writes of our need to persevere with a loved one who is considering Christ.

At each stage you have to be willing to go along with him at God's speed, which may seem to you a strangely slow speed. But that is God's business, not yours. Your business is simply to keep pace with what God is doing in his life. Your willingness to be patient with him in this way is the proof of your love to him no less than of your faith in God.[2]

HAULING IN HOLY MACKEREL

While we're waiting for the fish to bite, let's look at principles of fishing.
■ Put it in words.
Make the Gospel clear. Because you've been a Christian for some time and have lived your faith alongside those you love, it's easy to think that they know what you're about. Have you actually sat down with your parents, with your child, with a loved friend, and spelled out the basics of the Gospel?
Think back. When your mom was in the hospital for an operation, you got "serious" about her salvation. What happened? Did you ever broach the subject again after she was back on her feet? Your child prayed a sinner's prayer, mouth mimicking yours, when he was seven. Have you followed up on that child's commitment during his teenage years?
It's easy to conclude that the fish aren't hungry when, in fact, there's no bait left on the hook. Pull in your line and tie

on some fresh bait before casting it back out in the water.
■ Expect the hometown treatment.
Parents find it difficult to take their children's opinions seriously. Whether Dad has been in investments and now Junior offers him advice on mutual funds, or Mom has been the resi-
dent counselor and is now challenged by her psychologist son,
parents naturally resist the "authority" of their children. Similarly, children defend themselves against their parents' ideals
in order to carve out an identity of their own. Even neighbors
who see a gangly teenager return home with a family of his
own have trouble seeing him as a full-fledged adult.

When the subject is faith, this resistance comes up strong.
We spread the contents of our Christianity on the kitchen table
only to receive rolled eyes, uncomfortable sighs, and raised
eyebrows from those we thought would be most interested.
We return for the holidays and turn cocktail chatter to Christ
and our old high school buddies stare at us in disbelief.

When Jesus stood to address the hometown folks in the
synagogue in Nazareth, His familiarity bred contempt.

"Where did this Man get this wisdom and these miracu-
lous powers?" they asked. "Isn't this the carpenter's
son? Isn't His mother's name Mary, and aren't His brothers James, Joseph, Simon and Judas? Aren't all His sisters with us? Where then did this Man get all these
things?" And they took offense at Him (Matthew 13:54-
57).

Jesus wasn't a boy on the verge of manhood, testing His
knowledge against His superiors. He didn't throw out opinions
to be discussed, to be considered, to be weighed by those in
authority over Him. Jesus claimed that He had *the truth*. He
proclaimed His words to be God's words, and people who
knew Him as a barefooted youngster didn't like it. "Only in his
hometown and in his own house is a prophet without honor,"
was Jesus' reply. When you give the good news of the Gospel
where you are known, expect the hometown treatment.

■ Show and tell.

There are all kinds of suffering in life. One decidedly difficult path of pain is the unequal yoke of a Christian married to one who does not share the faith. In Peter's instructions for suffering in a way that honors Christ, he includes this situation. The fishing tips he offers for the married can apply to any relationship with unsaved loved ones. Peter challenges us to win folks to the Word with the same spirit of quiet submission with which Jesus faced death.

> Wives, in the same way be submissive to your husbands so that, if any of them do not believe the word, they may be won over without talk by the behavior of their wives, when they see the purity and reverence of your lives (1 Peter 3:1-2).

Second, after you've created curiosity about Christ, prepare to meet it with information. "Always be prepared to give an answer to everyone who asks you to give the reason for the hope that you have. But do this with gentleness and respect" (1 Peter 3:15).

Peter's version of evangelism suggests that we hold our answers until others ask the questions which arise from a natural process of watching our lives. Some Bible students call this the "show and tell" passage on evangelism. First we show our faith to our loved ones and then we tell them what it is they're seeing and how they can have it too.

■ Team up.

Some things are better done in teams than alone. The writer of Ecclesiastes points out the benefits of teamwork as support, comfort, and strength—all factors necessary to get the job done.

> Two are better than one, because they have a good return for their work: If one falls down, his friend can help him up. But pity the man who falls and has no one to help him up! Also, if two lie down together, they will keep

warm. But how can one keep warm alone? Though one may be overpowered, two can defend themselves. A cord of three strands is not easily broken (Ecclesiastes 4:9-12).

This truth is illustrated in the account of Jesus and the paralytic (Mark 2). Jesus was in a house in Capernaum, ministering to the crowd that had gathered. So many had congregated that there was no room left, not even outside the door. When the paralytic's four friends realized that they were unable to reach Jesus, they carried their friend to the roof and, removing the boards, lowered him down on his bed into the presence of Christ.

This was a relatively simple task, because Palestinian homes were constructed with an exterior stairway leading from the ground to the roof. The roof was made of clay and mud, supported by large beams set about three feet apart. Grass grew on top of this structure. Joining minds and bodies into a singular purpose, these men found a way to carry their paralytic friend to Christ.

You've watched loved ones limp toward God and then stop halfway there. Perhaps a physical problem barred their way, or maybe they couldn't get past an emotional barrier. As you've watched, your own faith weakened. It seemed they'd never make it. You offered an arm, a lift, a direction, and you sensed that these would not be enough. More was needed— more than you had to give alone.

Mark gives us a practical principle for bringing such people to God: team up. Pray that God will provide another believer in the life of your unsaved loved one. Ask Him to plant a Christian coworker, a Christian doctor, a Christian neighbor alongside the one you've been nudging toward Christ. As Jesus said, "One sows and another reaps (John 4:32)." In order to get our loved ones into the kingdom of God, it often takes a team approach.

■ Give it a rest.

There comes a time in fishing when you've followed all the

advice of the experts and need to just sit back in the boat with one hand on the line and wait. Some call this step relinquishment. In *Parents in Pain,* John White defines this as "giving your children (or any loved one) back to God and in so doing remembering to take your own hands off them."[3]

When we meet the dead-end realization that we cannot make someone we love trust Christ, and that salvation is a decision between him and God, we have no choice but relinquishment. We cannot enter that sacred room of commitment for another or coerce him into the kingdom. A.W. Tozer describes this process of relinquishment in his book *The Pursuit of God.*

> We are often hindered from giving up our treasures to the Lord out of fear for their safety; this is especially true when those treasures are loved relatives and friends. But we need have no such fears. Our Lord came not to destroy but to save. Everything is safe which we commit to Him, and nothing is really safe which is not so committed.[4]

God loves those we love even more than we do and we can trust them to Him. If anyone can bring them into the kingdom, He can.

GIVE IT TIME

Earl Palmer, pastor of First Presbyterian Church in Berkeley, California, comments, "Evangelism, like sanctification, takes time. Therefore, we must take the time it takes."[5] Some fish are so eager to be caught that they need only a bit of bait and they're in the boat. Catching them is both easy and fulfilling. But such hauls can deceive us.

Most fish are not such easy prey. They mull over their options. The stakes are big. They need time to consider the commitment. Fishing for these creatures requires a lengthy excursion into the deep. There, lines trolling out behind a huge motorized boat, we sit strapped into seats and scorched by the sun, waiting for the lurch on the line.

Finally we feel the tug. He's hooked. We set ourselves to battle him into the boat. After hours of laborious reeling in and letting out, we sight him at the surface. And oh, the temptation to loosen our grip, to relax our stance! Then, without warning, he hurls his body out of the water and dives down deep, ripping the line through our gloved hands, burying our hopes in a watery grave.

We sit down and begin the winding process over again. The sun sets and we relinquish the responsibility for the catch to others and go below to rest and dream of the fish. When morning comes, we return to our position once more, waiting, winding, wondering when the fish will give in.

Evangelism takes time. And if we're serious about seeing our loved ones converted to Christ, we must spend the time it takes to stick with the questions they ask over and over again, to couple our words with our deeds, to refuse the tug-of-war between pushing harder and withdrawing altogether. We must bait up our hooks, cast them in the water, and then we must wait.

> The truth is that the work of evangelizing demands more patience and sheer "stickability," more reserves of persevering love and care, than most of us twentieth-century Christians have at command. It is a work in which quick results are not promised; it is a work, therefore, in which the non-appearance of quick results is no sign of failure; but it is a work in which we cannot hope for success unless we are prepared to persevere with people.[6]

It's up to us to fish. We are to get in the boat, offer the bait, and wait. When the fish don't bite we're to stay in the boat, offer fresh bait, and wait. When the fish still don't bite we're to remain in the boat, change the bait again, and continue to wait. But we must not forget this one thing:

With the Lord a day is like a thousand years, and a thousand years are like a day. The Lord is not slow in keeping His promise, as some understand slowness. He is patient with you, not wanting anyone to perish, but everyone to come to repentance (2 Peter 3:8-9).

It's up to us to fish. It's up to God to get them to bite.

7

WAITING
for the Crop to Come In

When I was in kindergarten, we planted marigold seeds in Dixie cups. Then we waited. It seemed like those seeds would never grow. I put my miniature garden in our kitchen windowsill. Each morning I sprang from my bed to check its progress. It always looked the same—brown, muddy dirt in a cup. I remember begging my mother to let me dig up the seed to see whether it was doing anything in the dark. She said that if it was growing, digging it up would stop the growing process.

Just when I was ready to toss my Dixie-cup garden in the trash, a brave sprout pushed its way out of the soil, raised its head over the cup's edge to the sunny window.

Between our attempts and our accomplishments is a gap called waiting. We punch down the seeds for our careers, marriages, children, and self-growth into the soil of our lives, water them, and then wait for growth. When we've done all we can, we sit like farmers, waiting for the crop to come in.

SEASONAL GROWTH

The Bible tells us, there is a "time for everything, and a season for every activity under heaven" (Ecclesiastes 3:1).

83

Just as there are seasons of growth during the year, there are seasons of our lives. In each developmental stage of adult life, certain results are expected. Whatever seasons we are in, we find ourselves waiting for a crop to come in.

■ Spring is the planting season.

In spring, rains come and soften the winter-toughened turf. Robins lay eggs in thatchy nests, animals mate, and we punch seeds down into the ground.

We can liken spring to the coming of age of a young man or woman. When a youth leaves the parental home to make a new one, to hold down employment, to build relational foundations in friendship and marriage, he or she is giving birth to a new person: an adult. Out of the shadows of his semiformed life, an identity is born.

Even in a day when the line between adolescence and adulthood is more blurred than ever before, most psychologists pinpoint the late teenage years through the late twenties as the seasons of identity formation. In her book, *Passages,* Gail Sheehy calls it a time of "taking hold of the adult world by mastering what you're supposed to do."[1]

Spring is the time for planting the seeds of who you're going to be. Once the crop is planted, you move on to the next stage in life's cycle of growth: summer.

■ Summer seems to happen overnight.

We move through the spring of the twenties and suddenly arrive at summer: thirty. Richard Cohen, a syndicated columnist for *The Washington Post,* writes of how he discovered his own adulthood.

> Several years ago, my family gathered on Cape Cod for a weekend. My parents were there, my sister and her daughter too, two cousins and, of course, my wife, my son and me. We ate at one of those restaurants where the menu is scrawled on a blackboard held by a chummy waiter and had a wonderful time. With dinner concluded, the waiter set the check down in the middle of the table.
>
> That's when it happened. My father did not reach for

the check. In fact, my father did nothing. Conversation continued. Finally, it dawned on me. Me! I was supposed to pick up the check. After all these years, after hundreds of restaurant meals with my parents, after a lifetime of thinking of my father as the one with the bucks, it had all changed. I reached for the check and whipped out my American Express card. My view of myself was suddenly altered. With a stroke of the pen, I was suddenly an adult.[2]

Summer is the season of tending the garden of our lives. From the challenge of creating an identity, we transition to finding a place for who we've discovered we are. Gail Sheehy observes that adults in the summer of life are asking, "What do I want out of life, now that I'm doing what I'm supposed to do?"[3]

We survey the crop we've planted and decide what to nurture and what to uproot. As psychologists put it, we choose a niche for our lives and work at it. Then, we sit back and wait for our garden to grow.

■ Autumn days wear into coolness as dark approaches.

The fruit drops lush and full from the vine. We enter the garden swinging empty baskets and return with backs bent from the abundance of the crop. We wash and peel, shuck and scrub, can and freeze, and share with family and friends. At last, harvesttime is here.

In the autumn of mid-life, the days grow shorter. As the temperature drops, we realize that winter is coming, that the promise of spring lies two seasons behind us. As psychologist Daniel Levinson puts it, "What we are losing is much more evident than what we may gain."[4]

Autumn's task of reviewing achievements and redirecting remaining energies leaves many of us disillusioned and even panicky. We ask questions like, "What is the purpose of life? Is this all there is? Does life begin at forty, or is forty just the beginning of the end?" We wait for results with more intensity than ever before. What grows or doesn't grow seems to describe the success or failure of our lives.

■ Winter is a season of stillness.

In its whitewashed serenity, when we go to the pantries of our lives and pull out the bounty of our spring, summer and autumnal efforts. Human developmentalist Maggie Scarf highlights the task of winter. "The flavor of this period of life is now of discovery: who one was and what one did are reviewed; this is a phase of final consolidation."[5]

Consolidation means different things for different people. As they look back, some people find unfinished business and rush out to complete what they can in the days that are ahead. Others find their own lives in a state of disarray and hurry to tidy them so that the task won't fall to their children after they're gone. Still others, who find their own lives in order, look outwards in continued giving, creating even more memorials to the messages of their lives.

While the winds of winter howl outside, we stay securely within the walls of home, rummaging through the cupboards, pilfering the pantry, and enjoying the bounty we've brought in. Thumbing through scrapbooks of the past, preparing final legacies for future generations, ordering personal effects, we draw ever closer to the Source of hope for the future. Here the wait is for last-minute changes and the final call to home.

THE GARDEN AT MID-LIFE

The season of autumn, or mid-life, presents a unique challenge because it is so focused on results. For this reason it deserves further attention. When September and October roll around, the garden is supposed to deliver. The past, the present and the future define themselves by the harvest of autumn. Waiting for results is a pastime uniquely intense for those in mid-life.

■ Now or never.

Time, which was previously our ally, betrays us to the enemy's side. A "now or never" mentality directs our thinking. We kneel in the garden of our lives, inspecting the soil for signs of growth. We want to know *now*. Was it worth it? Did it matter? Do we continue? Or give up?

Roger Gould, a psychiatrist and researcher at the University of California at Los Angeles, observes that in mid-life,

> . . . we see more clearly, and consequently we are more frightened. For we know that we *must* act on our new vision of ourselves and the world. The desire for stability and continuity which characterized our thirties is being replaced by a relentless inner demand for action. The sense of timelessness in our early thirties is giving way to an awareness of the pressure of time in our forties. *Whatever we must do must be done now!*[6]

Our bodies, our bosses, and our children relay messages that we're no longer young. As Haddon Robinson, president of Denver Seminary, writes,

> The middlescent lives life between sunrise and sunset. He numbers his years not in terms of birth but of death. Instead of marching forward from birthday to birthday, he looks at the number of years until deathday. In the middle years we are shaken by the reality that we are finite and mortal.[7]

Aging and death are no longer events we'll somehow avoid. We see them in the distance, creeping closer. We can't wait any longer for results! If the crop doesn't come in, and come in now, we won't be around for the harvest!

■ So what?

In panic, we search for answers. We look back to the seeds we planted in our youth: our marriages, our children, and our work. At the center of the search is our self: the person we've become over the years. We gaze over the garden of our lives and begin the evaluation process. So now, what about my life?

Some seeds have matured into towering trees of success. In spite of their height, we wonder if they couldn't have been healthier, stronger, somehow better. Our children are grown, but what will they accomplish with their lives? Our careers have brought in a decent pension, but what do we have of eternal worth as a result of our involvement in them?

Other seeds have produced only average or subaverage seedlings. Despite careful pruning, fertilizing, weeding, and waiting, their growth has been slow.

A few seeds are still marked with a stake, but their growth is invisible, even after all these years. We remember the day we planted them, full of hope and expectation: the stocks we bought for the kids' education, the singing ministry we began as a young couple, the new company we organized with high hopes, the evangelistic meetings in the neighborhood, the quiet witness we shared with friends. Now we glance their way and wonder if they'll ever bear fruit in our lifetime, or even in the lifetimes of our descendants.

Then we look forward. How much more can we yet accomplish with our lives? How much more height will we see added to the tall trees? Will the seedlings soon mature? Will those unseen seeds we've babied reward our patience with growth? Should we shift our efforts, planting new at this late date?

Perhaps the most perplexing quality about this autumnal inspection is that even when we find signs of growth in our lives, we're not sure how to evaluate them. Sally Conway describes the mid-life dilemma of the average man.

> Life is like a pile of important papers someone has tossed into the air that the breeze from a nearby fan tosses and tumbles even more. As they fall and scatter on the floor and under the furniture, he has to bend down and gather them up. As he does, he realizes he is tired, dizzy, and discouraged. He has to sort and reorganize the papers and decide if some should be discarded or rewritten.[8]

The wait for results is trying at any time, but particularly difficult for those in autumn who are ready to harvest and retire on the return. When the crop doesn't come in by the desired date, we're tempted to dig up the seeds and forget farming.

HOW DOES YOUR GARDEN GROW?

The Bible offers help for those who are waiting for the crops to come in. Jesus talks about seeds and soil, about gardeners and vines, about sowers and reapers. While not many of us make our living off the land, we do respond when God's Word lands where we live.

We endure our waiting for results by cooperating with the gardener. When we participate with God in the growth process, we invite Him to share the harvest fruits of godly character, of healthy family relationships, of meaningful ministry and rich labor in our lives and in the lives of those around us.

■ God as gardener.
Jesus' Parable of the Sower speaks of God as the Gardener.

> This is what the kingdom of God is like. A man scatters seed on the ground. Night and day, whether he sleeps or gets up, the seed sprouts and grows, though he does not know how. All by itself the soil produces grain—first the stalk, then the head, then the full kernel in the head. As soon as the grain is ripe, he puts the sickle to it, because the harvest has come (Mark 4:26-29).

The point of the parable is this: growth is up to God. Whether it occurs in spring, summer, fall, or not at all, growth is God's responsibility. Paul points to this truth in relation to the church: "I planted the seed, Apollos watered it, but God made it grow" (1 Corinthians 3:6). And in Galatians 5, he describes the fruit of the Spirit as the result of the Holy Spirit's work in our lives.

Telly Monster is a fucshia-haired creature who lives on Sesame Street. In one scene, singer Smokey Robinson finds Telly surrounded by piles of food. With all the effort he can muster, Telly groans, strains, stretches, and pulls his blobby body upwards. In between exercises, he stuffs his mouth with food. When asked what he's doing he replies, "I'm trying to grow."

You and I are a lot like Telly Monster. We grunt and groan, trying to grow ourselves into what we think God wants us to be when all along, He's at work in us, growing His image into our personality.

Cooperating with God through life's growth cycles means accepting His identity as the gardener. We can encourage God's growth process in us through prayer, obedience, and Bible study. But in the end, God is responsible for all spiritual progress in us through the power of His Holy Spirit. There comes a time when we've done all we can to help ourselves and our dreams grow and we must wait while He brings fruit from the seeds He has set in our lives.

■ Ourselves as garden.

The second principle for cooperating with God through life's growth cycles is to accept that we are the garden. While we can't control our growth, we can actively participate in the growth process by preparing the soil of our lives to receive God's Word and by enduring God's pruning process.

● Preparing the soil. The Parable of the Sower tells of a farmer who scattered seed a handful at a time across a wide expanse of earth. Since in biblical days, paths cut right through fields, seed fell on both hard-packed earth and receptive terrain. Some seed naturally fell into areas where it could not grow.

Jesus describes four kinds of soil, each representing a listener's response to God's Word.

Listen! A farmer went out to sow his seed. As he was scattering the seed, some fell along the path, and the birds came and ate it up. Some fell on rocky places, where it did not have much soil. It sprang up quickly, because the soil was shallow. But when the sun came up, the plants were scorched, and they withered because they had no root. Other seed fell among thorns, which grew up and choked the plants, so that they did not bear grain. Still other seed fell on good soil. It came up, grew and produced a crop, multiplying thirty, sixty, or even a hundred times (Mark 4:3-8).

This parable compares soil types to people. Ask yourself if you have ever received the seed of God's Word—have you trusted Jesus for salvation?

To get the maximum from the parable, consider your soil type as your stage of maturity in Christ.

What kind of soil are you? As God plants the seed of His Word down into your life, does it fall on a hard-packed heart? Does the seed of God's Word have a chance to get down into the soil of your life, or are you so indifferent to His desires that it's carried off the surface?

Does God's seed land on the rocky soil, a thin layer of dirt just above a shelf of limestone, where nothing can take root? Did you once draw near to God, finding relief and compassion in His presence only to pull away when the trying times hit, concluding that He was no God you wanted to follow?

Does God's seed find a spot of soil between the thorns and there take root only to have its fruit choked and stunted? Was there a time when you sincerely trusted Christ and began a relationship with God, but somehow other things became more important? Your job, your marriage, your children, your dreams and desires now choke out the crop God intended to harvest from the soil of your life.

Or does God's seed land in good soil, in a soft place, tilled up and ready to nourish its lessons and take them to heart? As you listen to God's Word, do you learn? As you learn, do you share? As you share, do you grow and do others around you enjoy the fruit God produces in your life?

What kind of soil are you? God is the Gardener. He plants the seed. He makes it grow. But we can cooperate with Him by being receptive soil, receiving the Word He plants in us even when we don't expect or desire it, or even understand it. We can help bring in the crop by being the kind of soil in which something good can grow.

● Enduring the pruning. Once the crop begins to grow, it must often endure pruning in order to bear fruit. Each year I plant petunias in the flowerbeds around our house. And each year I struggle over what I know must be done.

I always fight with myself at this point. If I leave the blossoms affixed, I can immediately enjoy their beauty. Yet, I run the risk of producing scrawny stems and meager blossoms by midsummer. If I pinch off the blossoms, I will miss the glory of immediate results while ensuring a display of color all summer long.

Slowly, almost begrudgingly, I begin the pruning process, opting for faith over sight. When I'm done I'm left with rows of naked green plants, and a tug in my heart. Jesus taught about pruning.

I am the true vine, and My Father is the Gardener. He cuts off every branch in Me that bears no fruit, while every branch that does bear fruit He trims clean so that it will be even more fruitful. You are already clean because of the word I have spoken to you. Remain in Me, and I will remain in you. No branch can bear fruit by itself; it must remain in the vine. Neither can you bear fruit unless you remain in Me (John 15:1-4).

New Testament scholar William Barclay reports that the cultivation of a vineyard is one of the most time-consuming and attention-demanding kinds of farming. Vines creep so fast that the slips are initially set in the ground twelve feet apart. Then young vines are not allowed to fruit for their first three years. Each year they are cut back in order to conserve their life and energy.

Cooperating with our Gardener means enduring the pruning process. This takes faith. We cringe at the sight of God's clippers. Snip. Snip. Snip. "Not that part!" we call. "Not so short!" we beg. "Please leave that long one intact," we bargain.

"I am the vine and My Father is the Gardener." Jesus

knows what needs to go and what needs to stay. All that
would hinder our growth is cut away while all that nourishes
His image in us stays. We cooperate with God in the growth
cycles of life by recognizing His role as Gardener and ours as
garden and as such, by preparing our soil and enduring the
pruning process.

GROWTH BENEATH THE GROUND

Spring is a season for planting the seeds of identity. In
summer we tend the gardens of our dreams. Autumn sends us
to the fields to harvest. And in winter we want to lean back
and enjoy the bounty. When the seasons of life don't match up
with the almanac's predictions, we can learn to delight in the
continued growth of the yet unharvested. Speaking to students
at Princeton University, Adlai Stevenson once commented,

> What a man knows at fifty that he did not know at twenty
> boils down to something like this: the knowledge that he
> has acquired with age is not the knowledge of formu-
> las . . . but of people, places, actions—a knowledge not
> gained . . . by words, but by touch, sight, sound, vic-
> tories, failures, sleeplessness, devotion, love—the hu-
> man experiences and emotions of this earth; and perhaps
> too, a little faith and a little reverence for the things you
> cannot see.[10]

While you're waiting, delight in what God is growing. Send
your roots deep and drink from the streams of His living
Word.

Whether in a Dixie cup or in the garden of our lives, seeds
grow in the dark over a long period of time. Resist the urge to
dig them up. While you're waiting for your crop to come in,
cooperate with the Gardener.

Blessed is the man who trusts in the Lord,
whose confidence is in Him.

Waiting for the Crop to Come In

He will be like a tree planted by the water
that sends out its roots by the stream.
It does not fear when heat comes;
its leaves are always green.
It has no worries in a year of drought
and never fails to bear fruit (Jeremiah 17:7-8).

8
WAITING
for Another Chance

The wind dug up the waves and tossed them against the ship. Tilting to one side and then the other, the boat dipped her bow beneath the next onslaught. Ropes groaned and boards creaked. Somewhere up above the din, a deafening crack sounded as the mast broke away. Sailors hurled crates and barrels overboard, lightening the load. Between curses at the wind and waves, they begged their gods for mercy.

Below deck, one man slept. Wrapping guilt about himself like a warm blanket, he hid in the privacy of his dreams.

"How can you sleep?" the captain's bellowing interrupted his catnap. "Get on your knees and ask your God to spare us!"

The fugitive pulled himself up on one elbow, shaking away the slumber-haze and its safety. Across the cabin, everyone drew a stick out of a pouch. Then they turned en masse on the man who had drawn the shortest stick. "It's you! You're responsible for the calamity of this storm! Who are you? What are you running from? Tell us the whole story!"

Jonah drew in his breath. "I am a Hebrew and I worship the Lord, the God of heaven, who made the sea and the land. The Word of the Lord came to me, telling me to go to Nineveh."

Jonah waited for a reaction. Getting none, he continued,

"But I refused! The Ninevites are despicable! Whether in battle or in peace, they plot evil against Yahweh. They practice witchcraft and prostitution. They wipe men out like ants. I won't be used to get them off the hook! They deserve Sheol, and worse!"

Jonah's words flew about the cabin, but only a few registered. They heard that Jonah was somehow connected to the God who controlled the sea. One sailor questioned, "What should we do to you to make the seas calm down again?"

"Throw me overboard," Jonah directed. "The storm is a result of my disobedience."

Though afraid, the sailors were not heartless. Strapping themselves onto what was left of the ship's railing, they stabbed oars at the waves in one last attempt to reach shore. Finally, they conceded that their only choice was to follow Jonah's directive. They hoisted him over the side and watched his body disappear in the churning sea.

Onboard, the decks leveled. The swaying masts righted themselves. The wind silenced, and grateful sailors offered thanks to the God of Jonah. Peace returned to their world.

But Jonah's storm continued. A great fish rose up and swallowed him whole. For three days and nights, the fish carried Jonah in its belly where he was schooled in the lessons of his failure. During those long, dark days, Jonah was forced to wait for a second chance. When you're in the belly of a whale, you can't do much else.

A COURSE DESCRIPTION OF FAILURE

Like Jonah, we assume we know the surest path to success. We slip out the back door of obedience and trot off toward the good times. And like Jonah, we too fail. God gives us a command and we ignore it, believing His way is harsh, risky, time-consuming or just not fun.

■ Our view of failure.

How we respond internally to failure depends on our personalities and our life experience.

Some of us absorb our failures. When we make mistakes, we let them define us. Our self-confidence plummets and our energy erodes. We accept the criticism and judgment of others as our just reward. But the judgment of another isn't enough, so we condemn ourselves.

For many, failure means worthlessness. It's not that we *make* mistakes. We conclude we *are* mistakes. We regard a second chance as undeserved. A future of any kind is too much to expect. Failure is not something we *do,* it's something we *are.* We see no option for another chance. We are what we are, and we can't change that.

Others of us deny failure. Quickly, we set to work, building a new pedestal to display our worth. Waiting for another chance seems a humiliating inconvenience. Some people can expect to suffer, but not us! With a stubborn spirit of independence, we refuse to submit to the lessons of failure. They have nothing to teach us. As John F. Kennedy once remarked, "Success has many fathers, but failure is an orphan; no one wants to claim it."

■ God's view of failure.
God takes a radically different view of our failures. He separates our being and our doing. While He knows we will *make* mistakes, He knows that we *aren't* mistakes.

Failure is not necessarily the opposite of success but is, rather, a means of achieving success. As Dr. Vernon Grounds, president emeritus of Denver Seminary, writes,

> The Bible turns values topsy-turvy, puts on top the things fallen man puts on the bottom, and ranks last things fallen man puts first. It praises weakness which is strength and denounces the strength which is weakness. . . . No wonder then, that it praises the failure which is success and denounces the success which is failure.[1]

God's view of failure can be summed up in two statements. First, God expects us to fail. In his book *Another Chance,*

Dean Merrill writes that God "has been watching over a planet of imperfect children for a very long time. What we have done was hardly a shock to Him. He has seen it many times before.[2]

Speaking of the ease with which we err in what we say, James writes, "We all stumble in many ways. If anyone is never at fault in what he says, he is a perfect man, able to keep his whole body in check" (James 3:2). God expects us to fail.

Second, God uses failure for His purposes. The familiar words of Romans 8:28-29 illustrate God's central purpose for the lives of those who love Him.

> And we know that in all things God works for the good of those who love Him, who have been called according to his purpose. For those God foreknew He also predestined to be conformed to the likeness of His Son, that He might be the firstborn among many brothers.

In God's mind, success equals Christlikeness. He pledges to use all things, even failure, to achieve this definition of success in the lives of those who love Him. As Paul Billheimer points out, "The flesh may doubt this, but no matter how much a man succeeds, if he does not develop lofty, sublime, Godlike character, he has failed both in time and in eternity."[3]

We tend to define character by what we do. When we fail, our doing is worthless and we conclude that our character is also without value. God, on the other hand, evaluates character by being. When we *do* wrong, He hates our sins, but He still loves and values the personhood of those who are related to Him through Jesus Christ.

IN THE CLASSROOM OF FAILURE

Nineteenth-century physicist Sir Humphrey Davy once said that the most important of his discoveries were suggested to him by his failures. More recently, Thomas P. Watson, president and CEO of IBM, offered this formula for success: "Double your rate of failure—failure is a teacher. A harsh one, but the best."⁴

■ Failure teaches us about ourselves.
When we stop ignoring failure and let it teach us, we can learn lessons about ourselves. For example, failure reminds us that we are finite creatures who will make mistakes. No matter how obsessive and compulsive we are about keeping our houses clean, meeting deadlines at work, pleasing people, parenting perfectly, or praying consistently, we will fail.

In addition, failure illustrates what doesn't work. When we try to carry three bags of groceries at once and two of them rip, we learn that saving time may mean making more trips to the trunk of the car. When we watch our spouse's wounded face, we learn that berating words won't heal the rift between us. English author John Keats wrote,

> Failure is, in a sense, the highway to success, inasmuch as every discovery of what is false leads us to seek earnestly after what is true, and every fresh experience points out some form of error which we shall afterward carefully avoid. ⁵

Further, failure reveals what we have yet to give up to God. As Paul Billheimer puts it, "Failure may be necessary to beat the stiff backbone of self-confidence out of us."⁶ When we're forced to see our failures and our response to them, we learn how far we have to go with God. He doesn't. We work to impress Him with expensive gifts of perfect performance even when they're way out of the budget of our behavior. Failure convinces us that we can't save ourselves. In Psalm 119:67, David admits, "Before I was afflicted, I went astray, but now I obey your word."

■ Failure teaches us about God.
In failure we have a unique opportunity to know God. Like black against white, our failures contrast with God's constancy, and teach us truths about Him. First, God's being doesn't fail. God is utterly reliable. Zephaniah 3:5 says, "The Lord

within her [Jerusalem]) is righteous; He does no wrong. Morning by morning He dispenses His justice, and every new day He does not fail." Shortly before he died, Moses said to the children of Israel, "Do not be afraid or terrified of them [the enemies of Israel], for the Lord, your God goes with you; He will never leave you nor forsake you" (Deuteronomy 31:6). The same is true for us today. God is utterly reliable.

Second, God's love doesn't fail. No matter what we do or don't do, when we know Jesus Christ as Saviour, nothing can separate us from the love of God. While we were still sinners, Christ died for us. The unconditional love stemming from the heart of God is a love which cannot be altered, no matter how awful our errors.

■ Failure teaches us about our need for God.
When we fail, we clearly see ourselves, our God, and the gap between us. Failure points out our inadequacies and our great spiritual need.

There's a financial term to describe when a person runs out of financial resources: *bankruptcy,* which conveys the idea of being broken, ruined, depleted, destitute, or impoverished. When he comes to the end of himself and faces the fact that he owes a debt he cannot pay, a man perceives only one way out—to declare bankruptcy.

The Greek language uses two words for *poverty.* One expresses the idea of a destitute person who lives hand-to-mouth. A stronger word conveys the idea of one who possesses nothing at all, and who, despite his best efforts, can provide nothing for himself or his family.

It is the second, stronger word that Jesus used when He said, "Blessed are the poor in spirit, for theirs is the kingdom of God" (Matthew 5:3). The poor in spirit realize their complete spiritual lack before God. They acknowledge that they have nothing to offer the Ruler of the universe. They testify to their total inability to provide for their need. They openly declare themselves spiritually bankrupt before the One to whom they owe such a great debt.

When we harm our marriages, insult our children, step on

others on the way up the ladder, and disregard the needs of those around us, we fail. But our failures can teach us about our need for God. In the black days of guilt, we can discover that our resources are not great enough to cover our mistakes. Seeing that, we're made ready to receive payment from another Source: God. Jesus paid the price for our sins; He covered our debt by dying for us on a cross. He alone has the resources to meet our debt because He is God.

CHECKPOINTS FOR REENTRY

How do we know when we've learned the lessons of failure? When is our learning about ourselves, our God and our need of God completed to the point that we're ready to graduate—ready for another chance?

Interviews and research reveal three common checkpoints for reentry after failure. Whether your failure is a result of deliberate sin or human insufficiency resulting from sin in general, you may wonder when you're ready to step back into the active life.

■ Grace has done its work.

We begin on our knees—no, on our faces. Prostrate before God in the utter humiliation and sorrow of confession, we are "willing to die."⁷ Barely able to move our lips, we whisper the words of our sin, hoping that verbal confession will bring relief.

> When I kept silent, my bones wasted away through my
> groaning all day long.
> For day and night Your hand was heavy upon me;
> my strength was sapped as in the heat of summer.
> Then I acknowledged my sin to You
> and did not cover up my iniquity.
> I said, "I will confess my transgressions to the Lord"
> —and You forgave the guilt of my sin (Psalm 32:3-5).

In the simple act of bringing words of repentance before a forgiving God, grace begins its cleansing work that runs down through three layers of our lives.

● Grace restores us spiritually. Nicholas, the first Czar of Russia, would occasionally dress himself as an army officer in order to observe the military routine from the inside. He had a favorite soldier, the son of an intimate friend, whom he had placed in charge of the monies used for soldiers' salaries.

The young man fell into bad habits and over time gambled away a huge sum from the government funds. One night he received notice that an official would be by the next morning to examine the records and count the money he had on hand. The soldier went to the safe, drew out the measly amount left and sat down to make calculations as to how much was missing. After playing with the figures for a while, he wrote under the numbers, "A great debt; who can pay?"

In utter despair, he concluded that there was no way he could ever settle, and he made up his mind that in the morning he would put a loaded revolver to his temple. In spite of the horror of the situation, he was suddenly overcome by drowsiness and slept.

While he slept, Czar Nicholas, dressed as a soldier, entered the room. A quick glance at the spilt coins, the figures, and the exhausted slump of a soldier and he surmised the situation. His first thought was to arrest him. The next moment his heart went out in compassion. He glanced down, saw the pitiful question, "A great debt; who can pay?" and scrawled a word in reply. He sealed the paper with his ring and left.

After about an hour, the soldier awakened and saw that it was long past midnight. He grabbed the revolver, lifted it—but before he could pull the trigger, his eye caught on a word written on the sheet of paper: "Nicholas." He knew it was not there when he went to sleep. And next to the signature was the seal of the Czar's ring. The soldier compared this signature with official versions he possessed. "The Czar has been here tonight. He knows all my guilt, and yet he has undertaken to pay my debt. I need not die!"

When you were dead in your sins and in the uncircumcision of your sinful nature, God made you alive with Christ. He forgave us all our sins, having canceled the written code, with its regulations, that was against us and that stood opposed to us; He took it away, nailing it to the cross (Colossians 2:13-14).

The common Greek word for the cancellation of a contract is *chiazein,* which means to write the Greek letter *chi* (X) across a document. Thus, the debt was "crossed out." However, in Colossians 2, Paul uses the Greek word *exaleiphein,* which means "to wash over" or "to wipe out." In New Testament times, the ink used was a mixture of soot and gum diluted with water. While it was lasting and durable, a wet sponge could wipe ink off the slate, leaving it clean for reuse. Thus, when Paul writes that our sins have been canceled, he means they have been wiped out, rubbed off the page. They no longer stand in writing to condemn us.[8] "To confess your sins to God is not to tell Him anything He doesn't already know. Until you confess them, however, they are the abyss between you. When you confess them, they become the bridge."[9]

● Grace restores us relationally. Whether our failure has affected marriage, family, workplace, church, or people we barely know, we can verify our readiness for reentry into real life by looking for harmony in our relationships.

In some cases relationships are stronger after failure than before. In other situations, a permanent rift rises which cannot be resolved. In both cases, God's grace works to restore peace in the one who has wronged others. We can't make others forgive our blunders, but we can live out our forgiveness toward them.

Two behaviors illustrate that grace has worked to restore relationships. On the one hand, we release resentment. Our feeling of resentment is an inevitable result of being damaged and wounded with the words or actions of another. Even when we've instigated the hurt, it boomerangs back at us and we experience it ourselves. To try to squelch the bitterness and pain that comes when we've been hurt is to deny our human ability to feel.

But we don't have to welcome resentment as a permanent member of the family. Forgiveness means releasing resentment. Forgiveness soothes the pain of offense. If we want the healing it promises, we must experience it on both a mental and emotional level. Recognizing and owning our emotions, and refusing the negative feelings of resentment, is demanding but necessary work.

> Suppressed resentment will never die; it will be held in reserve and nurtured like malignant toadstools in the cellar. Resentment suppressed will never lose its power, like a spark in a gasoline tank, a bit of momentary friction will set off a devastating explosion.[10]

When we've failed, relational restoration comes as we release resentment. We can either permit bitterness to take permanent root in our hearts or we can act to release it.

Another behavior which illustrates the work of God's grace in our relationships is that we choose love. As God chose to love us when we weren't exactly lovable, we who are recipients of His work of grace choose to love others. It takes God's example and His effort to convince us that we can love again. As His grace seeps through the soil of our sin, we commit to staying instead of going, to accepting instead of rejecting, to giving instead of receiving. When we've been loved, we can choose to love.

God's grace works first to restore us spiritually and then relationally as it encourages us to release resentment and choose love.

● God's grace restores us personally. In order for grace to be truly effective to us, we must be convinced we are forgiven. It is this which tells us we are ready for reentry and that grace has given us another chance.

You can prove your readiness for reentry by answering one question: "Have you forgiven yourself?" Not sure? Check inside your heart. Do you have an appropriate response to guilt?

God has placed guilt in human hearts to convict us of sin. He uses it as an arrow to pierce through our tough shells and to reveal our need for Him. An appropriate response to guilt is to let it lift our gaze from our sin to God's grace.

Godly sorrow brings repentance that leads to salvation and leaves no regret, but worldly sorrow brings death. See what this godly sorrow has produced in you: what earnestness, what eagerness to clear yourselves, what indignation, what alarm, what longing, what concern, what readiness to see justice done (2 Corinthians 7:10-11).

Still not sure? Look for another quality. Do you remember to forget your failure? In his book *Grace Is Not a Blue-Eyed Blond,* R. Lofton Hudson points out how hard it is to forget failure.

People bury hatchets but carefully tuck away the map which tells where their hidden weapon lies. We put our resentments in cold storage and then pull the switch to let them thaw out again. Our grudges are taken out to the lake to drown them—even the lake of prayer—and we end up giving them a swimming lesson. How often have we torn up the canceled note but hung on to the wastebasket that holds the pieces.[11]

The Bible writes a different definition of forgetting failure. "For as high as the heavens are above the earth, so great is His love for those who fear Him; as far as the east is from the west, so far has He removed our transgressions from us (Psalm 103:11-12).

By God's example, forgiving means forgetting. It means tying back the hand that longs to open a scab, so that the wound can heal. It means refusing to dwell upon wrongs that have already been righted.

Forgiveness means remembering to forget. That's what God does and that's what we must do for ourselves. If grace has completed its work in your person, you've forgiven yourself.

How do you know that the wait is over? That you've learned the lessons of failure and are ready for another chance? The first checkpoint is a conviction that grace has done its work. You've experienced—not just thought about but experienced—a spiritual, relational and personal restoration.

● Encouraging words are heard. A second checkpoint is that we finally start hearing and believing the positive comments made by those near to us. In failure, we doubt our most trusted beliefs. We see our strongest strengths as weaknesses. We flinch at the prospect of the future, fearing we have nothing left to offer our world.

Alongside us come comforters, friends housing God's Holy Spirit. They sweep up the fragments of our vanishing visions and preserve them for us until we have the faith to dream again.

Barnabas did this for John Mark. During Paul and Barnabas' first missionary journey, John Mark abandoned his responsibility in ministry and hightailed it home. Paul refused to take John Mark along on their second trip, and so Barnabas, whose name is really a nickname meaning "Son of Encouragement," took John Mark on a Gospel journey himself.

Near the end of his life, writing of his need for items in prison, Paul included John Mark in his letter, saying, "Get John Mark and bring him with you, because he is helpful to me in my ministry" (2 Timothy 4:11). Years later, John Mark served as God's instrument for penning the action-packed Gospel we call the Book of Mark. Barnabas' encouraging words not only provided John Mark with his second chance but convinced Paul to give him another opportunity as well.

When we're deafened by the shouts of self-condemnation, encouraging words simply don't register. Our own negative accusations interrupt another's positive comments. But when grace has done its work, convincing us of God's forgiveness, we hear what others have been saying all along. We have something to offer. We can make a difference! God has a place for us! Suddenly we catch the vision they've been carrying for us. We adopt it once more as our own and go on.

■ We are ready to take a chance again.
A third checkpoint is a readiness to risk. Where once our own needs were so great we could see no one else's, now the needs of others seem greater than our own. Measuring our offerings next to their needs, we calculate the risk.

The risk remains a risk. We could fail again. We could be rejected. We might appear foolish or miss the mark. But we're convinced that God has made us new. We believe again that we've been given something worth offering back. We see the need and we want to meet it.

And in such moments, we heed the inner prompting which directs us, "Don't wait. Start now. Forget the past. Embrace the future."

THE GIFT OF ANOTHER CHANCE

Since the time of our first father and mother our God has offered another chance to those who have failed. Many who thought they had flunked out of life for good reentered and graduated with honors. History tells of those who learned from their failures and became successful. Jonah was one. After he learned the lessons of failure, God gave him another chance. Deep in the belly of the whale, Jonah searched for a grip among the slippery entrails. Perhaps he remembered David's words.

Where can I go from Your Spirit?
Where can I flee from Your presence?
If I go up to the heavens, You are there;
If I make my bed in the depths, You are there.
If I rise on the wings of the dawn,
if I settle on the far side of the sea,
even there Your hand will guide me,

Your right hand will hold me fast (Psalm 139:8-10).

The far side of the sea—that's where Jonah had headed to escape God's command. His destination had been his mistake. Surely, the God who pronounced judgment on the Ninevites for their evils toward Him would just as easily snuff out the life of a disobedient servant. Nineveh. . . . He felt the light of his life blown out, darkness crushing his chest.

Nineveh! Reality found its roots in Jonah's confused thinking. He had refused to go because he knew Yahweh to be a God of mercy and compassion! He feared that God would not judge but would forgive—and he had wanted no part of such a God!

When my life was ebbing away, I remembered You,
Lord,
and my prayer rose to You, to Your holy temple.
Those who cling to worthless idols
forfeit the grace that could be theirs.
But I, with a song of thanksgiving,
will sacrifice to You. What I have vowed
I will make good. Salvation comes from the Lord
(Jonah 2:7-9).

After God commanded the fish to deposit Jonah on land, "the word of the Lord came to Jonah a second time." A second time to Jonah—and to Moses, and to Samson, and to David, and to Peter, and to John Mark. Using our sin, our failure, as a great teacher, the word of the Lord also comes to us a second time, offering another chance.

In 1929, Georgia Tech played the University of California in the Rose Bowl. In the first half, a man named Roy Riegels recovered a fumble for the University of California but became confused and ran in the wrong direction. Were it not for a teammate who outdistanced him and downed him, he would have scored for the opposing team. As it was, Tech capitalized on the blunder and scored a touchdown.

At halftime, Riegels, huddled in a blanket in the locker

room, put his face in his hands, and cried like a baby.

Coach Nibbs Price looked at the team and said simply, "Men, the same team that played the first half will start the second." All the players headed back out to the field—all but Riegels who remained in a heap on the floor. Coach Price hollered at him, "Didn't you hear me? The same team that played the first half will start the second."

Riegels looked up, responding, "I can't do it. I've ruined you. I've ruined Southern California. I've ruined myself. I couldn't face that crowd in the stadium to save my life."

Then Coach Price put his hand on Riegels' shoulder and said to him, "Roy, get up and go on back; the game is only half over." And Roy Riegels went back and played football as no man had ever played football.

We have a God of the second chance. He not only restores us but recycles our failures, using them for His purposes. His view of success is our conformity to the image of Christ. Failure can be the best preparation for this kind of success, if we will submit ourselves to its lessons while we wait for another chance.

All who are waiting for another chance, come to the God of the second chance! Enroll in failure's lessons and learn from this great teacher.

In the bitter waves of woe,
Beaten and tossed about
By the sullen winds that blow
From the desolate shores of doubt,
Where the anchors that faith has cast
Are dragging in the gale,
I am quietly holding fast
To the things that cannot fail.
And fierce though the fiends may fight,
I know that truth and right
Have the universe on their side;
And that somewhere beyond the stars
Is a love that is better than fate.

When the night unlocks her bars
I shall see Him—and I will wait.
                    —G. Washington Gladden

9
WAITING
for Answers

Why doesn't God give us what we want?
James says, "You do not have, because you do not ask God." It's true. We don't. The most obvious answer to the question, "Why doesn't God give us what we want?" is that we don't ask.

PRAYING WITH ABANDON OR ABANDONING PRAYER?

It's been said that we live in a nation that has taken prayer out of its life. What's true for our nation is also true for many individuals.

Prayer is one of the great boons of the Christian life. Through prayer we can actually talk to the God of the universe. We realize we're not alone in life. We receive help for our daily needs and derive strength for enduring challenges. If prayer is so rich in rewards, why don't we pray?

■ Help not wanted.

Many of us don't pray because we don't think we need it. Before we rush out the door in the morning we brush our teeth and gargle. We slam down juice and toast. We kiss the family and grab the report for the day's meeting—but we don't pray. Bad breath may cost us a client. Forgetting an important report could be embarrassing. At ten o'clock our stomachs will growl if we fail to feed them. But what difference will it make in our day if we don't pray? What visible evidence will betray us?

As I walk down the hall at church a friend stops and asks me to pray about an upcoming job interview. I say I will, walk away, and forget. Why? My husband tells me he expects an especially difficult day and asks for prayer. I assure him I will remember. He walks out the door, and his request is swallowed up in the pressing needs of my own day. Why?

Underneath our forgetfulness in prayer is the belief that we really don't need to pray. When we see a car coming at us head-on, we pray. When our child's screams tell us he's hurt, we pray. When our father, or husband, or wife, or sister lies dying in the hospital from a heart attack or a life-threatening disease, we pray. In crises, we see our human power pale, and we make a stab at trusting God. But we figure that we can handle the everyday matters on our own. We don't pray because we don't think we need to.

■ Question marks.

Another reason we don't pray is that we don't know how. We aren't sure how to approach God. Slipping down on our knees feels awkward and unnatural. Folded hands and bowed head make us feel childish.

When we finally position ourselves to ask for help, the words won't come. What do we say? Is there a formula to follow? We remember the acrostic ACTS from our days in Sunday School—Adoration, Confession, Thanksgiving, and Supplication. If we skip adoration and go straight to supplication, will God hear our needs? If we leave out thanksgiving, must we begin again? Must we punctuate our sentences with Thee and Thou?

And what, exactly, are we to ask for? Can we let God know we'd rather have a silver car than a red one? Do we dare ask for rent money by the fifteenth instead of the end of the month? Should we tell God we want to be married by our thirtieth birthday? Is complete health too much to ask, or should we request only strength to bear the pain of our afflictions?

Then comes the matter of how many times we should pray a prayer. Is once enough? When the Bible tells us to "pray constantly" or "to pray without ceasing," what does it mean? Do we chant our prayer in a monotone voice like those who follow cults? Is God so forgetful that we must remind Him of our needs? Must we approach and reapproach Him with our desires until we finally get Him on a good day or wear Him down on a bad day?

How long should we pray? David Brainerd spent entire days in prayer in the forests of New England where he was evangelizing the Indians. Martin Luther once remarked, "I have so many things to do that I cannot get along without three hours a day in prayer." George Washington supposedly went to his library at four o'clock each morning for devotions. Where would we fit such blocks of prayer into our overly busy lives?

■ Return to sender.

Yet another reason we don't pray is that we don't get answers. Perhaps this is most frustrating. We construct our sincere prayers, consistently offer them in the right posture using the correct formula, and still nothing happens. We receive our best supplications back, stamped: "Return to Sender."

In some instances, the Bible is very clear why our prayers aren't answered. Psalm 66:18 speaks of unconfessed sin: "If I had cherished sin in my heart, the Lord would not have listened." Similarly, Isaiah explains how sin affects Israel's relationship with God: "Surely the arm of the Lord is not too short to save, nor His ear too dull to hear. But your iniquities have separated you from your God" (Isaiah 59:1-2).

In some way, sin interrupts the flow of our requests to God and His response to them. One reason our prayers aren't answered is unconfessed sin.

James offers two other obstacles to answered prayers. In James 4:3 he suggests that selfishness obstructs our prayers. "When you ask, you do not receive, because you ask with wrong motives, that you may spend what you get on your pleasures." God refuses to stand in line behind other interests. In James 1:5-8, faithlessness is mentioned as a hindrance to prayer.

> If any of you lacks wisdom, he should ask God, who gives generously to all without finding fault, and it will be given to him. But when he asks he must believe and not doubt, because he who doubts is like a wave of the sea, blown and tossed by the wind. That man should not think he will receive anything from the Lord; he is a double-minded man, unstable in all he does.

God doesn't answer our prayers because we don't possess the faith to stick with Him until He does.

We don't have because we don't ask. Okay—so we finally work up the nerve to ask, and then nothing happens. We run down the list of "biblical obstacles to prayer." What sin have we overlooked? Where have we been selfish or faithless? When our prayer comes back stamped "Return to Sender," we feel like giving up.

WHY GOD WITHHOLDS

You've prayed for thirteen years for your missionary friends in Pakistan. They've yet to participate in one conversion.

For a year and a half, you've prayed that God would open up a fulfilling job opportunity for your husband. While you're grateful for any money, you wonder why all he can find is a job flipping hamburgers.

As your nest empties, you watch your children fly off to lives of their own. From infancy, you've prayed for their salvation. Out of four, only one has made a decision for Christ.

Your father has had three strokes in two years. As soon as he improves, his body cruelly sets him back with another. He can't talk. He can't move. His body is but a shell housing his spirit. The pain of his wounded pride peaks out, begging for release. You've prayed both for healing and for death, as you plead with God for mercy. But each day his condition remains the same.

We don't have because we don't ask, or because we ask wrongly: sinfully, selfishly, faithlessly. Is that it? Is unanswered prayer all our fault?

If prayer is "collaboration with God," as John White puts it, or "conversation with God," as Rosalind Rinker defines it, then it is by nature, two-way. Where two are involved in communication, two are responsible for an apparent break in communication.

Our prayers may go unanswered because of us. But the silence may be God's doing as well. Sometimes God withholds what we think we want in order to give us what He knows we need.

■ **God withholds so we'll want Him.**
God knows we need Him, and sometimes the only way to convince us of this fact is to withhold what we think we want. George MacDonald puts it this way.

What if He knows prayer to be the thing we need first and most? What if the main object in God's idea of prayer be the supplying of our great, our endless need—the need of Himself? . . . Hunger may drive the runaway child home, and he may or may not be fed at once, but he needs his mother more than his dinner. Communion with God is the one need of the soul beyond all other need. And some need is the motive of prayer. . . . So begins a communion with God, a coming-to-one with Him, which is the sole end of prayer, yea, of existence itself. . . . We must ask that we may receive, but that we should receive what we ask in respect to our lower needs is not God's end in making us pray. For He could give us everything without that. To bring His child to His knee, God withholds that man may ask.[1]

God knows that what we really need is more than what we

115

want. So He withholds what we want so that we'll be drawn to Him. When we lack, we feel our need. Haddon Robinson writes, "While God in His grace does give good gifts to His children, He offers us more than that. He offers us Himself. Those who are merely satisfied with the trinkets in the Father's hand may miss the best reward of prayer."[2]

■ God withholds so we'll want what He wants.
There's another reason why God withholds. We don't always know what's good for us, but God does. He refuses to give us what might bring us harm.

We go about our days hunting for the good times and the safe times, praying for release from lousy circumstances through the arrival of easier moments. C.S. Lewis suggests,

> We want, in fact, not so much a Father in heaven as a grandfather in heaven—a senile benevolence who, as they say, "liked to see young people enjoying themselves," and whose plan for the universe was simply that it might be truly said at the end of each day, "a good time was had by all."[3]

Hansen's disease, the modern-day term for leprosy, attacks the nervous system and destroys the victim's ability to feel pain. As a result, those suffering with it can damage their bodies unawares. Without knowing it, a victim might grab an object too tightly, walk around on a blister-infected foot, or strum a guitar until a finger falls off.

Medical technicians have experimented with devices which provide an electric shock whenever a vulnerable part of a victim's body is being abused. But often when engaged in an activity that might bring about abuse and, therefore, the shock, patients will switch off the device to avoid the sensation.

There seems to be a conflict between what will make us immediately comfortable and what will make us eventually Christlike. And God is too good to make us comfortable when, in comfort, we might lean away rather than toward Him.

Again, I appeal to C.S. Lewis:

> It is for people whom we care nothing about that we demand happiness on any terms: with our friends, our lovers, our children, we are exacting and would rather see them suffer much than be happy in contemptible and estranging modes. If God is Love, He is, by definition, something more than kindness. . . . He has paid us the intolerable compliment of loving us, in the deepest, most tragic, most inexorable sense.[4]

Prayer is God's tool of change. God uses prayer to align our desires with His. As Richard Foster puts it, "Prayer is the central avenue God uses to transform us."[5] Similarly, Soren Kierkegaard commented, "Prayer does not change God, but it changes the one who offers it."

God alone knows what is best for us. Through prayer, He communicates what He knows to us. Through both granting and withholding our requests, God makes us good. God sometimes withholds what we want so we'll want what He wants.

MAJOR PRAYERS FROM A MINOR PROPHET

"How long, O Lord, must I call for help, but You do not listen?" (Habakkuk 1:2) Habakkuk's words echo our thoughts. While the details of our days are different, all who've approached God in prayer relate to his feeling that God's ears are deaf.

Like us, Habakkuk wrestled with God in prayer. He questioned God's silence and doubted God's wisdom. When God withheld what Habakkuk wanted, he negotiated for a partial settlement. When God said no, Habakkuk satisfied himself with what God wanted to give—Himself.

Habakkuk wanted God to discipline wayward Israel. His book opens with Habakkuk waiting for an answer and expressing his frustration with not having one. God gives an answer but not the one Habakkuk expects. In fact, Habakkuk finds it incomprehensible. God is going to use the pagan Babylonians to punish a people more righteous than they: Israel.

Head reeling, Habakkuk questions God's wisdom. This isn't what he requested! How could God be so careless, so unfair? Couldn't He think of another way?

God responds to Habakkuk's request with an assurance that Babylon will get her due and that Habakkuk, like all of Israel, should exhibit a trust in the character of Yahweh. He will withhold what they want in order to give them what they need.

Habakkuk then reviews God's well-established pattern of trustworthiness and readies himself for the fulfillment of God's words.

We only have three short chapters of Habakkuk's conversations with God, but they contain major principles of prayer.

■ Pray with a willingness to wait.

Habakkuk questions God's plan for disciplining Israel through Babylon and then settles in, waiting for God's answer. "I will stand at my watch and station myself on the ramparts; I will look to see what He will say to me, and what answer I am to give to this complaint" (2:1). Like a guard who waits through his watch with eyes peeled for a sign of movement, Habakkuk waited for God.

The first principle Habakkuk teaches is that we must pray with a willingness to wait. Similarly, we must wait on God with a willingness to pray. Waiting and praying go together. Like two shoes of a pair or two halves of a whole, they work as a team. In his book *Desiring God,* John Piper writes,

> The folly of not waiting for God is that we forfeit the blessing of having God work for us. . . . God aims to exalt Himself by working for those who wait on Him. Prayer is the essential activity of waiting for God: acknowledging our helplessness and His power, calling upon Him for help, seeking His counsel.[6]

If we want results from our prayers, we must pray with a

willingness to wait. In her book *Adventures in Prayer,* Catherine Marshall compares prayers to eggs, saying, "Prayers, like eggs, don't hatch as soon as we lay them."

■ Pray with honesty.

The Hebrew word for prayer meant "cutting flesh." Praying with a willingness to wait doesn't mean sitting in mental or emotional numbness. While we wait, we can be honest. And yet, it is here that we cringe. Will God tolerate an uncut version of our thoughts and feelings? We picture God rubbing weary eyes, grimacing over our weaknesses, throwing up hands in disgust. We're too pushy, too whiny, and He walks away from our pleas altogether. Surely a cloak of pious faith is better than honesty!

Contrary to our worst fears, God delights in our honesty in prayer. When we admit we cannot go on without Him, without what He wants in our lives, He rejoices. Habakkuk cried out, "How long?" stripping himself of his neat prophetic robes and laying bare his impatience and frustration. When he got an answer he didn't like, he questioned it. He didn't hide his human doubts but displayed them before the One who had the answers.

God wasn't shocked. He wasn't offended. He wasn't pushed to the point of anger. True, He withheld what Habakkuk requested, but He listened.

■ Pray with perseverance.

In Luke 11, Jesus taught His disciples to pray. After giving them the Lord's Prayer, He told them a parable.

Suppose one of you has a friend, and he goes to him at midnight and says, "Friend, lend me three loaves of bread, because a friend of mine has come to me, and I have nothing to set before him."

Then the one inside answers, "Don't bother me. The door is already locked, and my children are with me in bed. I can't get up and give you anything." I tell you, though he will not get up and give him the bread because he is his friend, yet because of the man's boldness he will

119

get up and give him as much as he needs (Luke 11:5-8).

We tend to think that we have to catch God at a weak moment in order to get our way. Like the neighbor in the parable, we assume that God won't give us what we want unless we force our way. The point of the parable is not that God must be caught off guard. It's not that we must find Him asleep and quickly take what we want before He awakens.

This parable teaches that we are to persevere in prayer. We are to continue praying for what we want over and over, keeping at it until we receive answers. As we bring our requests to God repetitiously, we partake of His presence repetitiously and give Him more opportunities to change our hearts. Frederick Buechner writes, "Be importunate, Jesus says—not, one assumes, because you have to beat a path to God's door before He'll open it, but because until you beat the path maybe there's no way of getting to *your* door."[7]

Along these same lines, John White points out, "We are to keep our prayers active not for God's memory but for our own."[8] Praying with perseverance gives God more opportunities to mold our desires to His.

■ Pray with readiness.

When we pray to God we must ready ourselves to receive his response. *His* response, not ours. In his classic book *Prayer*, O. Hallesby writes,

We plan the whole answer to our prayer. It seems so easy to us. In this particular situation we think that there can be only one thing for God to do if He is to answer our prayer. The answer must come now; it must come immediately. And it must come exactly the way we have planned it.[9]

While Habakkuk waits for God's response to his doubts, God speaks, warning that what He is telling is only part of what Habakkuk wants to hear. The rest will come when the time is right.

Write down the revelation and make it plain on tablets
so that a herald may run with it.
For the revelation awaits an appointed time;
it speaks of the end and will not be proved false.
Though it linger, wait for it;
it will certainly come and will not delay (Habakkuk 2:2-3).

God then describes the fall of Babylon. Purposely, He leaves out one detail: the date. He doesn't tell Habakkuk it will be in 539 B.C., 66 years after the prophecy. He leaves Habakkuk still needing to know. God wants him ready to act on His response. He's to ready a runner to deliver His message quickly so that Israel can receive the blessing of God's intentions.

We are to pray with readiness, ready to receive God's promised best, from whatever direction it comes, in whatever day He deems best. Ready or not, God's answers will come. As Jesus said, "When the Son of Man comes, will He find faith on the earth?" (Luke 18:8) Will we miss God's work, eyes glued only on our expectations? Or will we enjoy it because we're ready to receive it from wherever it comes?

■ Pray with confidence.
Stephen Olford tells of a spot on the Columbia River where a well springs up at low tide, offering clear, pure water for drink. Then the tide comes in and the spring is immersed. It's easy to assume that the spring has stopped flowing. But when you dive down, you can see a spout of clear, pure water still bubbling beneath the river's murky flow.

When we can't see what God's doing, only faith believes He's at work. Habakkuk believed. He received God's instructions to ready a runner, heard God's promise to one day destroy Babylon, and said, "That's good enough for me." He didn't know how or when God would accomplish His promise. But he didn't need to know.

The last of his three chapters sings of confidence in God. Habakkuk's praise centers on two truths. First, he exalts God's faithful actions. Habakkuk looks back, in 3:1-15, tracing

God's protection of His people from Egypt to Canaan. God's past acts of faithfulness in our lives motivate us to believe, even when there is no evidence of His present involvement.

Second, Habakkuk extols God's faithful character. Looking beyond what God once did, he sees a God who is worthy to be trusted and believed, even when He appears inactive. His words offer hope to us who wait for answers in our lives.

> Though the fig tree does not bud
> and there are no grapes in the vines,
> though the olive crop fails
> and the fields produce no food,
> though there are no sheep in the pen
> and no cattle in the stalls,
> yet I will rejoice in the Lord,
> I will be joyful in God my Saviour.
> The Sovereign Lord is my strength;
> He makes my feet like the feet of a deer,
> He enables me to go on the heights (Habakkuk 3:17-19).

Even when there was no evidence of God delivering what He had promised, Habakkuk prayed with confidence. Because he trusted in the faithfulness of God's actions and character, Habakkuk was surefooted, like the deer in high places. With a willingness to wait, honesty, perseverance, readiness, and confidence, Habakkuk prayed. The prayer of a righteous man is powerful and effective!

WAITING WITH ALL OUR MIGHT AND MAIN

We have not because we ask not. When we do ask, there are times we still don't have because God doesn't give. When you get down to it, we'll never completely understand prayer. On this subject, I imagine I'll still be staring at heaven and scratching my head until I die. The most sincere prayers can go unanswered while the apparent worst may bring results. Prayer is a mystery which even fervent faith can't unlock.

What we can know is that our God is a good God who loves us enough to withhold what we think we want, in order to give us what He knows we need. He withholds so we'll want Him and what He desires.

L.M. Montgomery wrote a tale of an enchanting redheaded orphan growing up in Canada. Impish and intrinsically curious, Anne of Green Gables focused her all on every moment the present brought her.

In one scene, Anne waits alone at the train depot, readying herself for her new adopted family, the Matthew Cuthberts. They are late and she is afraid. But she focuses her attention, as always, on the moment she is living and the task given her in it.

> The long platform was almost deserted; the only living creature in sight being a girl who was sitting on a pile of shingles at the extreme end. Matthew, barely noting that it *was* a girl, sidled past her as quickly as possible without looking at her. Had he looked he could hardly have failed to notice the tense rigidity and expectation of her attitude and expression. She was sitting there waiting for something or somebody and, since sitting and waiting was the only thing to do just then, she sat and waited with all her might and main.[10]

Waiting with all our might and main—that's what we can do as we look for answers to our prayers, because we know the God we're waiting on. And knowing Him makes all the difference. He is faithful to withhold what we think we want in order to give us what He knows we need.

10
WAITING
for the Mourning

Mr. Hairston didn't know he was going to die. Oh, he knew that he would die *someday*. What he didn't know was that the day of his death was only a few weeks away.

He entered the Veteran's Hospital a few weeks before Christmas for routine surgery. During the operation, the doctors discovered cancer. Then, to make matters worse, he broke two bones during recovery.

I met him on a Thursday in January, while I was doing an independent study—a special internship on death. At the Veteran's Hospital where I volunteered, Mr. Hairston fit my subject matter.

His ward was arranged like a military barracks, neat rows of metal beds saluting personnel and visitors alike. A nurse pointed out Mr. Hairston. He was a large man in his early sixties, ebony-skinned with peppery hair. As I drew nearer, despite his pain, he elbowed his bloated body to attention. Introducing myself, I entered the world of the dying.

In the days that followed, I relived Mr. Hairston's history, fed him his meals, fluffed his pillows, held his hand, prayed his prayers, and pondered his questions. My nights were weighted with his burdens.

Just two weeks after I met Mr. Hairston, he lost the ability to talk, to focus, and to be present. The medicine which prolonged his life robbed him of its enjoyment. His eyes, like windows to his soul, revealed confusion, fear and pain, warmth and understanding. He made no reply to my questioning. "Are you afraid? Do you know what is happening to you?" But when I asked if he wanted me to be quiet, or even to leave, his hand tightened in mine with an emphatic "No!"

On Friday, January 25, one of the hospital chaplains informed me that Mr. Hairston's condition had worsened. When I arrived at his bedside, I saw that he looked different. My eyes lingered on the tubes; the IV and catheter gave and then took the fluids of life. His breath came quickly in and out, in and out.

For several hours I witnessed a tug-of-war between life and death. A vacant look flickered across the familiar face of my friend, hinting at the struggle within. Every so often his eyes would open, register recognition and then fade shut again.

While I sat beside Mr. Hairston, a strange companion took up the death wait with me. It was a haunting prediction of the future, a ghostly goblin of my own inevitable departing. Mr. Hairston's finiteness mirrored my own and that of my friends, my family, and of everyone I'd ever known.

I wasn't at the hospital when Mr. Hairston died. It happened late that night when I was back in my dorm room going on with life. But I've never forgotten Mr. Hairston . . . not his life or his death.

We all know we're going to die. Some people know when, but most are surprised by death's silent approach. As we near death, we find ourselves waiting. For release? Yes, but also for the final period which ends our life sentence. Those solitary months, days, and hours preceding death are an exercise in waiting which none can really share with us. How will we respond to them?

Sitting with Mr. Hairston, waiting for his death, I learned something about life. The way we die is as important as the way we live. Our dying says as much about life as our living.

Both our living and our dying make up the message we leave behind.

OUR DENIAL OF DEATH

The Bible teaches that we all will die. From dust we came and to dust we will return.

> All men are like grass, and all their glory is like the flowers of the the field. The grass withers and the flowers fall, because the breath of the Lord blows on them. Surely the people are grass (Isaiah 40:6-7).

> You turn men back to dust, saying, "Return to dust, O sons of men." . . . You sweep men away in the sleep of death; they are like the new grass of the morning—though in the morning it springs up new, by evening it is dry and withered (Psalm 90:3, 5-6).

> Now listen, you who say, "Today or tomorrow we will go to this or that city, spend a year there, carry on business and make money." Why, you do not even know what will happen tomorrow. What is your life? You are a mist that appears for a little while and then vanishes (James 4:13-14).

In centuries past, men and women recognized their finiteness. Early Christians prepared for death, endeavoring to make a statement about life through it. The martyrs paid a high price for a few words for Christ. And when their tongues were silenced, their dead bodies were further testimonials.

French social historian Philippe Aries reveals that early Western man accepted death as his familiar, ordinary, and expected destiny. Prolonged death was considered a privileged state, allowing the dying an opportunity to prepare. Death was a public ritual organized by the dying person himself in his bedchamber with neighbors, family, and priest.[1]

Today, life and death are different. A "good" death is a sudden one which brings no warning and no pain. Why be warned and have to alter a carefree lifestyle when we can go out in a blaze of glory? We strip life of any association with death, hoping to avoid it altogether. We coin phrases like "expired," "departed," "asleep," "croaked," "kicked the bucket," "passed away," and "lost," to avoid the harsh reality of "dead." We move the dying from the home to the hospital, distancing ourselves from the inevitability of death's reach. In our youth-oriented culture, we assume we can avoid death through low-fat diets, vitamins, exercise, and medicine.

In *Wind River Winter,* Virginia Stem Owens points out that our earthly ties to death are being cut off. To grasp the reality of death in life, she directs our gaze outside of our environment which feels so permanent.

> Outside, the world itself dies every year. We have almost forgotten that. The sun withdraws its light, darkness overshadows the earth. The waters freeze and the leaves decay. We forget because we don't have to live in that world anymore. We have created our own world where we have as much light and heat as we desire—hot running water, and strawberries the year round. We exempt ourselves from the season of death that envelops the world outside our artificial environment. We live as though on an alien planet; this has become our imitation victory over death.[2]

Real life is full of death, and our denial won't change that.

DEATHBED PREPARATIONS

At some point in every person's life, the denial of death gives way to reality. Death may approach gradually as we take more pills than steps in a day. Or, death may come suddenly, like an uninvited guest crashing a party. Whenever it enters our days, it surprises us with its personal attention. We always knew we would die, but somehow we never expected death to come this way, at this time.

■ How the dying look at death.

The realization begins to take root, as your days are described more by the process of dying than by the process of living. You are waiting for death.

● You may feel anger. Death is never convenient. Nor is it welcome. Like the bothersome mother-in-law who comes for the winter, the presence of death irritates us. It points out our faults, rubbing our nose in our mortality.

You feel swindled, cheated, betrayed, robbed. How can death come now? Now, when life is so full, so meaningful? Now, when I am so needed here? Now, when I have so much left to do? Now, when I finally have time to enjoy life?

● You may feel loss. Death is the ultimate insult. It strips, rapes, and ravages human value. As a doctor I know points out,

No matter how we measure his worth, a dying human being deserves more than efficient care from strangers, more than machines and septic hands, more than a mouth full of pills and a rump full of needles. His simple dignity as a man should merit more.

Psalm 88 reflects the pain of the dying. Note the losses mentioned in its description.

Losses

O Lord, the God who saves me,
day and night I cry out before You.
May my prayer come before You;
turn Your ear to my cry.

Awareness of
God's presence

For my soul is full of trouble
and my life draws near the grave.
I am counted among those

Peace

129

who go down to the pit;
I am like a man without strength
I am set apart with the dead,
like the slain who lie in the grave,
whom You remember no more,
who are cut off from Your care.

Strength
Stature
God's
protection

You have put me in the lowest pit,
in the darkest depths.
Your wrath lies heavily upon me;
You have overwhelmed me with all Your waves.
You have taken from me my closest friends
and have made me repulsive to them
I am confined and cannot escape;
my eyes are dim with grief.

Blessing

Friends
Freedom
Hope

I call to You, O Lord, every day;
I spread out my hands to You.
Do You show Your wonders to the dead?
Do those who are dead rise up and praise You?
Is Your love declared in the grave,
Your faithfulness in destruction?
Are Your wonders known
in the place of darkness,
or Your righteous deeds
in the land of oblivion?

Divine
intervention

But I cry to You for help, O Lord;
in the morning my prayer comes before You.
Why, O Lord, do You reject me?
and hide Your face from me?
From my youth I have been afflicted
and close to death.
I have suffered Your terrors
and am in despair.
Your wrath has swept over me;
Your terrors have destroyed me.

Feeling of
acceptance

God's
pleasure

> All day long they surround me
> like a flood;
> they have completely engulfed me.   Safety
> You have taken my companions
> and loved ones from me;
> the darkness is my closest friend.   Companionship

Look at the losses! Death isolates the sociable, incapacitates the industrious, and makes dependent those who are self-sufficient.

● You may feel fear. Death is personal. When it's your turn, you go alone. No one goes with you. No one takes your hand and helps you through the door and then sits outside, winking reassurance while you adjust to your new surroundings.

To make matters worse, we know no one who has died and lived to tell of it. While we can read of death in Scripture and trust in the presence of Jesus through it, we must still pass through the valley of its shadow alone with no roadsigns to guide us.

Joseph Bayly cites four common fears of death in his book *The Last Thing We Talk About.* There is a fear of one's contribution to life ending, a fear of death's separation, a fear of becoming a burden, and a fear of abandonment during death's approach.

● You may feel hope. In your journey through the darkest hours of life which may lead to death, your greatest comfort may come in the hope of the hereafter. In place of your fears, God offers you the certainty of what waits for you: His presence.

More than a century ago, a man named John Todd wrote a letter to encourage an aunt who was dying. To soothe her anxieties, he reminded her of the way she took him in when the death of his parents left him orphaned.

My Dear Aunt—
I am sorry to hear that you are feeble, perhaps I should

say sick, and even that there is fear on your part that you are not to be better in this world. . . .

You remember that is is now thirty-five years since my father died, and left me, a little boy six years old, without a mother, without a home, and with nobody to care for me. It was then that you sent word that you would take me and give me a home, and be as a mother to me. . . . At length the day was set when I was to go to you, ten miles off. What a long journey it seemed to me! And I well remember how disappointed I was that, instead of coming for me yourself, you sent old Caesar, the great, fat, black man, to bring me to you. How my heart sunk when he came, and I was told that I was to ride on the horse behind him, sitting on the blanket! . . . So we set out, just before night. Caesar took my bundle of clothing before him, and me behind him, and (my little dog) ran beside us. But before long, before we got to your house, I began to feel tired. My legs ached, and I was tired of taking hold of Caesar. By-and-by the evening and the darkness came on, and I felt afraid. . . . Caesar, too, was so dark that I could not see him, and he jogged on without saying a word. He had no idea that I was afraid.

"Caesar, ain't we most there?" said I in my terror.

"Yes, when we have got through these woods we shall see the candle in the house."

"Won't they be gone to bed?" for it seemed to me it must be nearly morning.

"Oh no, they will be all ready to receive us."

But at last, after winding and turning, and going uphill and downhill, a long, long way, as it seemed to me, we came out of the woods, and then the stars shone; and I was told which light was in your house. And when we got there you came out, and you gently took me in your arms as Caesar handed me down; and you called me your 'poor little boy,' and you led me gently in; and there was the blazing, warm fire, the bright light, and the table spread, and the supper all waiting for me! . . . How you soothed me, and warmed me, and put me to bed in the strange room, and heard me say my prayers, and staid with me till I was fast asleep!

And now, my dear aunt, you see why I have recalled all this to your memory. Your heavenly Father will send for you—a dark messenger, it may be. And he will be your conductor, and carry you safely through the darkness of the way. He will not drop nor leave you, for he is a faithful servant. You need not feel afraid, for he knows the way, and will take you directly to your home. There the door will be open, and your dearest friend, the Lord Jesus Christ, will meet you and take you in, and the supper will be waiting and the fires of love burning, and the light and glory of his presence all seen. What a welcome you will receive!

At any rate, don't fear the dark passage, nor the dark messenger. Receive it all as the little child did, and you will find the home.

Ever, ever yours, most gratefully,
John Todd[3]

God promises eternal benefits after death for those who trust Jesus as their Saviour in life: a new body with none of the imperfections or inadequacies of our present bodies, continual fellowship with God, complete understanding of and resemblance to Christ, and a hereafter without sorrow, pain, injustice, war, or death.

In the thin hours of the night when you beg for morning, your hope in the hereafter may pull you on toward dawn.

■ Getting ready to go.

Dying hurts. Under its onslaught of anger, loss, and fear, you cling to the hope of the hereafter. But as you wait for death, you'll sense the need to act. You'll feel the urge to set things straight, to prepare yourself, to get ready to go.

You feel the fact that you won't be returning here and need to say good-bye. How do you want to say farewell to those you love? Would your wife appreciate a letter to remind her in the years to come of your love? Would your family members treasure a video or cassette message to encourage them in your absence, to share with little grandchildren yet to come? Is there someone you should call or write, ending a feud, forgiving an offense, mending a hurt, sharing your faith one last time?

Consider planning your own funeral, composing a last message to leave with those you love. When you select the liturgy, the music, the Scriptures, the participants, and the method and manner of burial, you'll provide a means to comfort the grieving you leave behind.

Give thought to creating a legacy through stewardship. Under a lawyer's careful supervision, wills and trusts can share possessions and valuables consistent with your values and desires. Provisions made for children, spouses, and other dependents communicate love when you're no longer able to.

Unclench your tight grasp on things and people. Fight off the pride which directs you to keep your feelings hidden. Put aside stubbornness and self-sufficiency and reach out while you still can. Say good-bye with love and honesty.

As you gradually turn your gaze away from this life, you'll find comfort and hope as you say hello to the next. Prepare yourself to meet God. Jesus left us some words to ready us for His Second Coming. Their tone helps us as we prepare for death.

Be dressed and ready for service and keep your lamps burning, like men waiting for their master to return from a wedding banquet, so that when he comes and knocks they can immediately open the door for him (Luke 12:35-36).

Dress and get ready for eternal service. Bathe in the springs of God's grace. Adorn yourself with the fresh apron of a clean heart. Quicken your eye to see the need of another as training for service to Jesus. Practice the posture of kneeling your attitude in obedience to Christ's lordship.

MOURNING PERSONS

Death comes and goes, leaving a hollow hole in its wake. The wait is over. Or is it? Those who've waited for a loved one to die find themselves ushered into the waiting room of mourning.

■ How the living look at death.
With a broken heart, we work to lift the heavy veils of mourning. What do you experience as you wait with grief?

● You may feel anger. Just as those who lay dying felt cheated by death's fast approach, those who are left behind suffer grief.

At first you may be shielded by shock. But as the days and weeks pass, the blur of indifference wears off and the sharp corners of anger and resentment cut deep. Weeping comes in uncontrollable fits. You rage for no apparent reason.

Such emotional abandon terrifies, shocks and embarrasses most Christians. How can we, who love God, feel so numb and indifferent to His gifts, so resentful, hateful and revengeful of what He's allowed in our lives?

● You may feel loss. Sometimes, the only release for the grief-stricken seems to be death itself. The only consolation, the return of what has been taken. The only future, the past.

Nicholas Wolterstorff's twenty-five-year-old son, Eric, died in a mountain climbing accident. Few deaths come according to our schedules, but Eric's was especially untimely. He was nearing the completion of a master's degree, and his future seemed to stretch out before him with promise. His death rocked the stability that all those who loved him had taken for granted. His father wrote, "The pain of the now more outweighs the gratitude of the once was."[4]

Love abandons us in grief. We stand suspended in time, while all around us life continues as if nothing has happened. We wonder, how can people go on buying groceries when one mouth will never again eat? How can the trees bud and the flowers bloom when one pair of eyes will never again enjoy their display? In *A Grief Observed*, C.S. Lewis wrote of the death of his wife, "Her absence is like the sky, spread over everything."

Even when a whole family grieves together, they are not together. Each sits in his own separate room of grief. Again, in Wolterstorff's words: "When someone loved leaves home, home becomes mere house."[5]

● You may feel fear. Panic hits as you consider the future. How will you support yourself? What will you do with the house? How will you raise your children? How will you survive without the love and support of the one you loved? Who will you be without the definition brought by that relationship?

You listen to the titles: widow, widower, orphan—and you feel that you no longer fit into the neat categories of our society. The future yawns out in front of you in terrifying perspective.

■ Going on.

Eventually, as you wait, you discover grief's vice grip on your heart beginning to relax. This heart, scarred by cutting, may actually be larger, not smaller; kinder, more compassionate, wiser, and with a more intense gratitude. The gap left by loss did not lead it to collapse but stretched its capacity. "Only the soul that knows the mighty grief can know the mighty rapture. Sorrows come to stretch out spaces in the heart for joy."[6] And in this same vein, Virginia Stem Owens concludes her *Wind River Winter* with:

> Loosening the grasp is never easy for our kind. We come into this world with our fingers curled and only slowly, by repeated practice, do we learn to open our hands. It takes a good deal of dying to get us ready to live. Sometimes we simply refuse. We'd rather harbor what little life we have than die and scrape out a larger space for the Spirit.[7]

Perhaps it's true, as some say, that grief never really ends.

It only changes—turns directions with time. For those who wait in mourning, the morning may never come as it did once upon a time. But it does come. And with it, life goes on.

RESTING IN PEACE

Rest in peace. It's an epitaph etched on tombstones, a blessing for the departed. Those who wait for death, and for the mourning following, can rest in peace by living in the stillpoints of life.

When Henri Nouwen talks about waiting on God, he describes man's task in life as twofold: we are to do for others and we are to be done for. Both are part of our assigned service to Christ. He looks to Jesus in the Garden of Gethsemane for insight into the waiting process and discovers that prior to the Garden, Jesus was doing *for* others; after the Garden, Jesus was done to *by* others. The combination of Jesus' acting and being acted upon together made up His vocation. He would not say, "It is finished," until both His action and His being acted upon were completed.[8]

In Nouwen's words I see two truths for those who wait for the mourning. First, there is just as much value in dying as there is in living. While we tend to devalue the still parts of life, God values them. He fulfills His perfect will for us just as much through our being done for as through our doing for others.

John Ruskin captures this truth in his essay "There is Music in a Rest."

There is no music in a rest but there is the making of music in it. In our whole life melody, the music is broken off here and there by rests and we foolishly think we have come to the end of the theme. God sends a time of forced leisure, sickness, disappointed plans, frustrated efforts, and makes a sudden pause in the choral hymn of our lives, and we lament that our voices must be silent, and our part missing in the music which ever goes up to the ear of the Creator. How does the musician read the rest? See him beat the time with unvarying count, and catch up the next note true and steady, as if no breaking place had come between.

Not without design does God write the music of our lives. Be it ours to learn the time, and not to be dismayed at the rests. They are not to be slurred over, not to be omitted, not to destroy the melody, not to change the keynote. If we look up, God Himself will beat the time for us. With the eye on Him, we shall strike the next note full and clear. If we sadly say to ourselves there is no music in a rest, let us not forget there is the making of music in it. The making of music is often a slow and painful process in this life. How patiently God works to teach. How long He waits for us to learn the lesson.[9]

There is just as much value in dying as in living, in resting as in playing a note.

Second, the way we die is just as important as the way we live. Just as our lives leave a message, so does our death. Dying reveals much of the meaning of life. Turning again to the writings of Virginia Stem Owens,

The world does not die in one day. It must live through its dying, moment by moment, day by day, week by week. But at each of those moments, days, weeks, more of its essential self, its skeleton, is revealed. One sees through the tree branches now to the far side of the creek. The grass and the split seedpods of the field flowers turn translucent. And we too. As we die, our skeleton emerges, the bare bones of ourselves on which the soft, corruptible flesh has lain.[10]

John Wesley was once asked the secret of the Methodist movement. He replied, "Our folks die well." Our death reveals our life. The way we wait for death is as important as the way we live life.

Even if you are not now, one day you too will wait for the mourning. Be careful not to overemphasize the importance of how you live and then neglect the way you die. Wait well in life and death so that you'll never look back and mourn your waiting.

11
WAITING
Well

We all wait. We wait for jobs, mates, and children. We wait for those we love to love Christ. We wait for results after our earnest efforts. We wait for another chance after we've failed. We wait for answers to our prayers. We wait for death and for the healing that mourning brings.

The way we wait reveals the extent to which we trust the One we are ultimately waiting for. How well do you wait?

While we'd like to wait well, the truth is that we usually don't! Waiting is inconvenient! We hate the helplessness it creates in us! We resent its waste of time! We reject its value!

But finally, when we've exhausted all other alternatives, we settle in to endure the wait. Yet somehow enduring it isn't enough. We who know and love God want to do more than simply endure the days He has ordered. The way we wait reveals the way we trust the One we're waiting for. If we want to show God we trust Him, we'll learn to wait well.

HOW TO WAIT WELL

Those who wait well have learned to express trust in God in their waiting times. Here are five principles for waiting well.

■ Think right: Give God room to work while you wait. Train your mind that God is working while you wait. What is this work? God is in the business of making us like Himself. Once we're born into the new life of a relationship with Him, He works to make us grow. One way we mature is through waiting. And when we wait, we allow God to do His work in us.

A saint's life is in the hands of God like a bow and arrow in the hands of an archer. God is aiming at something the saint cannot see, and He stretches and strains, and every now and again the saint says, "I cannot stand any more." God does not heed, He goes on stretching till His purpose is in sight, then He lets fly. Trust yourself in God's hands.[1]

God is in the business of making us like Him. He loves us too much to leave us the way we are. Instead, He uses circumstances, pleasant and painful, to mold our wills and our hearts to conform to His. And when we wait, we give Him room to work.

■ Stay present: Live to the fullest right now.

Forgive me, Father.
You gave me the
perfect gift of
right now,
and I threw it away
hoping for a better gift
later.[2]

Life can be full, even while we wait. Plant your focus in the present and keep it there. Instead of rushing through the present as if it didn't matter, pay attention to the lessons of the moment. Instead of cocking your head constantly to see what's "over there," learn that what is vital and important for you is taking place in the here and now.

Waiting well means living life now to the fullest. It means taking ourselves out of mothballs and using our talents, abilities and spiritual gifts. Robert Hastings challenges us to live fully in the present in his essay "The Station."

Tucked away in our subconscious minds is a vision—an idyllic vision—in which we see ourselves on a long journey that spans an entire continent. We're traveling by train and, from the windows, we drink in the passing scenes of cars on nearby highways, of children waving at crossings, of cattle grazing in distant pastures, of smoke pouring from power plants, of row upon row upon row of cotton and corn and wheat, of flatlands and valleys, of city skylines and village halls.

But uppermost in our conscious minds is our final destination—for at a certain hour and on a given day, our train will pull into the station with bells ringing, flags waving, and bands playing. And once that day comes, so many wonderful dreams will come true, and all the jagged pieces of our lives will fit together like a completed jigsaw puzzle. So, restlessly, we pace the aisles and count the miles, peering ahead, cursing the minutes for loitering, waiting, waiting, waiting for the station. . . .

"Yes, when we reach the station, that will be it," we cry. "When we're eighteen! When we buy that new 450 SL Mercedes Benz! When we put the last kid through college! When we win that promotion! When we pay off the mortgage! When we retire!" Yes, from that day on, like the heroes and heroines of a child's fairy tale, we will all live happily ever after.

Sooner or later, however, we must realize there is no station, no one place to arrive at once and for all. The journey is the joy. The station is an illusion—it constantly outdistances us. Yesterday's a fading sunset; tomorrow's a faint sunrise. So, shut the door on yesterday and throw the key away, for only today is there light enough to live and love. It isn't the burdens of today that drive men mad. Rather, it's regret over yesterday and fear of to-morrow. Regret and fear are the twin thieves who would rob us of that Golden Treasure we call today, this tiny strip of light between two nights.

"Relish the moment," is a good motto, especially when coupled with Psalm 118:24, "This is the day which the Lord hath made; we will rejoice and be glad in it."

So stop pacing the aisles and counting the miles. In-stead, swim more rivers, climb more mountains, kiss more babies, count more stars. Laugh more and cry less. Go barefoot oftener. Eat more ice cream. Ride more merry-go-rounds. Watch more sunsets. Life must be lived as we go along. The station will come soon enough.[3]

You may not be where you want to be, but you're still in a place worth living.

■ Watch out: Don't let waiting become a weak time. While you wait, raise your guard against the areas in your life most sensitive to invasion.

When you're waiting, it's easy to let your guard slip and become involved where you wouldn't otherwise. Have you ever noticed that x-rated magazines are readily available in the anonymity of airports? In the checkout lines at the grocery store, it's the most sordid gossip rags that hold the most marketable spots.

When you're waiting for a mate, beware of the beckoning of a relationship that promises intimacy without commitment. When you're waiting for a child, materialism woos, offering things as a replacement for a child. When you wait for answers to prayer, Satan may seem more present than God, whisper-ing lies of His abandonment. When the time for your wait has ended, the safety of the familiar can paralyze you from moving forward.

As you wait, watch out.

■ Give thanks: Close the complaint department. Jude 16 speaks of ungodly men who are "grumblers and fault-finders." The Greek word used here means "complaining about one's lot or cursing one's luck." It conveys the idea of blaming fate for tough circumstances. J.B. Phillips' rendition of Jude 16 reflects this meaning: "These are men who complain and curse their fate while trying all the time to mold life according to their own desires."

To complain is to grumble about your circumstances. It's to gripe, moan, and curse the substance and sequence of your days. And in so doing, it is to raise a fist at the One who set them in place.

There will always be a tension between what we possess and what we lack, between what God provides and what He withholds. Jim Elliot once wrote, "Let not our longing slay the appetite of our living."[4] It's easy to overlook what we have when we're out searching for what we don't have. Contentment comes when we abandon the search for what we lack and learn to live with what we have. Close the complaint department and give thanks.

■ Seek God: Learn to love God and not just His gifts.

How often we go to God with demands! Give me a husband by the time I'm twenty-eight and a baby when I'm thirty. Release me from my circumstances by Christmas!

In *A Grief Observed*, C.S. Lewis came full circle with his grief over his wife's death. He began by hammering his fists against a seemingly closed door in his prayers for her healing and ended with these words, "He can't be used as a road. If you're approaching Him not as the goal, but as a road, not as an end but as a means, you're not really approaching Him at all."[5]

It's easy to lose sight of God in the wait. Clarify the object of your wait. Are you waiting first for your wish list or for God? In Psalm 34:9-10, David concludes, "Fear the Lord, you His saints, for those who fear Him lack nothing. The lions may grow weak and hungry, but those who fear the Lord lack no good thing."

While God doesn't always give us what we want, He always gives Himself. Have we developed a desire to receive Him for who He is? Or will we turn Him away if He comes empty-handed without the precious merchandise we ordered?

FREEDOM WITHIN THE WALLS OF WAITING

Within her walls of waiting, Madame Guyon, a French noble-woman, found freedom. When she was only sixteen, she was married to a man twenty-two years older. In the short span between 1664 and 1676, she gave birth to five children and ushered a son, a daughter, a sister, her mother, and her father through death. After recovering from a serious illness in 1666, she contracted smallpox in 1670 and was left disfigured.

When her husband died in 1676, leaving her well-set financially, she devoted her attention to spiritual discoveries. As her insights grew, so did the popularity of her writings. In 1688 she was arrested and falsely accused of heresy, sorcery, and adultery by church officials who were jealous of her following. She was convicted and spent the next nine years in prison on these trumped-up charges.

Instead of grumbling against her wait, Madame Guyon found contentment as a captive. She wrote the following poem to express the freedom she found in waiting.

A Little Bird I Am

A little bird I am,
  Shut from the fields of air,
And in my cage I sit and sing
  To Him who placed me there;
Well pleased a prisoner to be,
Because, my God, it pleases Thee!

Naught have I else to do,
  I sing the whole day long;
And He whom most I love to please
  Doth listen to my song;
He caught and bound my wandering wing,
But still He bends to hear me sing.

Thou hast an ear to hear,
   A heart to love and bless;
And, though my notes were e'er so rude,
   Thou wouldst not hear the less;
Because thou knowest, as they fall,
That love, sweet love, inspires them all.

My cage confines me round:
   Abroad I cannot fly;
But, though my wing is closely bound,
   My heart's at liberty;
My prison walls cannot control
The flight, the freedom of the soul.

Oh, it is good to soar,
   These bolts and bars above,
To Him whose purpose I adore,
   Whose providence I love;
And in the mighty will to find
The joy, the freedom, of the mind![6]

The way we wait reveals the extent to which we trust the One we're waiting for. Waiting well means trusting wholly. Wait well—not because it's all you *can* do. Wait well because it's what God *asks* you to do.

What are you waiting for?

Endnotes

CHAPTER 1

[1]Mary Rice and Wendy Hofheimer, 1981, Birdwing Music/Cherry Lane.

[2]Dr. Robert Levine, "Waiting is a Power Game," *Psychology Today,* April 1987, 30.

[3]*Christianity Today,* 18 March 1988, 54.

[4]Ron Blue, *Master Your Money* (Nashville, Tenn.: Thomas Nelson Publishers, 1986), 13.

[5]Daniel M. Kehrer, "How to Cut Out Debt," *Changing Times,* 1 April 1988, 23.

[6]Helmut Thielicke, *The Silence of God* (Grand Rapids: Wm. B. Eerdmans Publishing Co., 1962), 14.

CHAPTER 2

[1]Paul E. Billheimer, *Don't Waste Your Sorrows* (Fort Washington, Pa.: Christian Literature Crusade, 1977), 59.

[2]Charles R. Swindoll, "The Temptation of Ministry: Improving Your Reserve,"

Endnotes

Leadership, Fall 1982, 19.

³C.S. Lewis, *A Grief Observed* (New York: Bantam, 1961), 4–5.

⁴Frederich Buechner, *Telling Yourself the Truth* (San Francisco: Harper & Row, 1977), 43.

⁵F.B. Meyer, *Moses* (Fort Washington, Pa.: Christian Literature Crusade, 1978), 26–27.

⁶Richard Foster, *Celebration of Discipline* (New York: Harper & Row, 1978), 91.

⁷Ruth Harms Calkin, *Tell Me Again, Lord, I Forget* (Elgin Ill.: David C. Cook, 1974), 95.

CHAPTER 3

¹*Rocky Mountain News,* 2 August 1987, 8.

²*Rocky Mountain News,* 26 August 1987, 10.

³Claudia Wallis, "Stress: Can We Cope?" *Time,* 6 June 1983, 50.

⁴Oswald Chambers, *My Utmost for His Highest* (New York: Dodd, Mead and Co., Inc., 1935), 214.

CHAPTER 4

¹Robert J. Havinghurst, *Developmental Tasks and Education,* 3rd ed. (NY: Longman Inc., 1972), 83–94.

²Cheryl Lavin and Laura Kevesh, "Tales From the Front," Chicago *Tribune,* January 1986.

³Carole Sanderson Streeter, *Reflections for Women Alone* (Wheaton, Ill.: Victor Books, 1987), 76.

⁴Rhena Taylor, *Single and Whole* (Downers Grove, Ill.: InterVarsity Press, 1984), 18.

⁵Luci Swindoll, *Wide My World, Narrow My Bed* (Portland: Multnomah Press, 1982), 170–171.

⁶Henri J.M. Nouwen, *Reaching Out* (Garden City, N.Y.: Doubleday and Co., Inc., 1966), 19.

[7]Harold Ivan Smith, *Positively Single* (Wheaton, Ill.: Victor Books, 1986), 21.

[8]Andrew Murray, *Waiting on God!* (London: James Nisbet and Co., 1900), 97.

[9]Dr. Connell Cowan and Dr. Melvyn Kinder, *Smart Women, Foolish Choices* (New York: Signet Books, 1986), 208–209, 211.

CHAPTER 5

[1]Mary Martin Mason, *The Miracle Seekers* (Fort Wayne, Ind.: Perspectives Press, 1987).

[2]Patricia Irwin Johnston, *Understanding: A Guide to Impaired Fertility for Family and Friends* (Fort Wayne, Ind.: Perspectives Press, 1983), 5.

[3]Beth Spring, "When the Dream Child Dies," *Christianity Today*, 7 August 1987, 30.

[4]Pam W. Vredevelt, *Empty Arms* (Portland: Multnomah Press, 1984), 7.

[5]Lynda Rutledge Stephenson, "What, No Kids?" *Partnership*, March–April 1987, 28.

[6]Lori B. Andrews, J.D., *New Conceptions* (New York: St. Martin's Press, 1984), 105–106.

[7]Mason, 39.

[8]Susan Jacoby, "Maternal Madness," *Vogue*, March 1984, 200.

[9]Andrews, 106.

[10]Michael Castleman and Daniel Ben-Horin, "In Search of Fatherhood: The Crisis of Male Infertility," *Redbook*, February 1985, 146–148.

[11]Stephenson, 27.

[12]Ann Kiemel Anderson, "God! Where Are You?" *Christian Herald*, November 1984, 59.

[13]Spring, 31.

[14]Johnston, 16.

[15]Johnston, 9.

Endnotes

CHAPTER 6

[1]Michael Cocoris, "Let's Go Fishing." Chapel talk presented at Denver Seminary.

[2]J.I. Packer, *Evangelism and the Sovereignty of God* (Downers Grove, Ill.: IVP, 1961), 121.

[3]John White, *Parents in Pain* (Downers Grove, Ill.: IVP, 1979), 165.

[4]A.W. Tozer, *The Pursuit of God* (Harrisburg, Pa.: Christian Publications, 1976), 28.

[5]Earl Palmer, "Evangelism Takes Time," *Leadership*, Spring 1984, 21.

[6]Packer, 119–120.

CHAPTER 7

[1]Gail Sheehy, *Passages* (New York: Bantam Books, 1977), 120.

[2]Richard Cohen, "Suddenly, I'm the Adult?" *The Washington Post*, 1986.

[3]Sheehy, 198.

[4]Daniel Levinson, *The Seasons of a Man's Life* (New York: Alfred A. Knopf, Inc., 1978), 9.

[5]Maggie Scarf, *Unfinished Business* (New York: Doubleday & Co., 1980), 468.

[6]Roger L. Gould, *Transformations—Growth and Change in Adult Life* (New York: Simon & Schuster, 1978), 217.

[7]Haddon W. Robinson, *Mid-Life* (Portland: Multnomah Press, 1982), 14.

[8]Sally Conway, *Your Husband's Mid-Life Crisis* (Elgin, Ill.: David C. Cook, 1980), 31–32.

[9]*Time*, 29 July 1966, 54.

CHAPTER 8

[1]Vernon Grounds, "Faith for Failure." Commencement address to Gordon Conwell Seminary, May 1977.

[2]Dean Merrill, *Another Chance* (Grand Rapids: Zondervan, 1981), 17.

[3]Paul E. Billheimer, *The Mystery of God's Providence* (Wheaton, Ill.: Tyndale

House Publishers, 1983), 79.

⁴Lisa Collier Cool, "Failure Can Be Good For You," *Cosmopolitan*, May 1986, 177–182.

⁵Ibid.

⁶Billheimer, 76.

⁷Merrill, 99.

⁸Merrill, 117–118.

⁹Frederick Buechner, *Wishful Thinking: A Theological ABC* (New York: Harper & Row, 1973), 15.

¹⁰Dan Hamilton, *Forgiveness* (Downers Grove, Ill.: IVP, 1980), 6.

¹¹R. Lofton Hudson, *Grace Is Not a Blue-Eyed Blond* (Waco, Texas: Word Books, 1972), 93.

CHAPTER 9

¹C.S. Lewis, *George MacDonald: An Anthology* (London: Bles, 1946), 51–52.

²*Focal Point,* Denver Seminary, January–March, 1987.

³C.S. Lewis, *The Problem of Pain* (New York: Macmillan Publishing Co., Inc., 1962), 40.

⁴Ibid., 41.

⁵Richard Foster, *Celebration of Discipline* (New York: Harper & Row, 1978), 30.

⁶John Piper, *Desiring God* (Portland: Multnomah Press, 1986), 140.

⁷Frederick Buechner, *Wishful Thinking: A Theological ABC* (New York: Harper & Row, 1973), 71.

⁸John White, *Parents In Pain* (Downers Grove, Ill.: InterVarsity Press, 1979), 232.

⁹O. Hallesby, *Prayer* (Minneapolis: Augsberg, 1931), 50.

¹⁰L.M. Montgomery, *Anne of Green Gables* (New York: Farrar, Straus & Giroux, 1908), 10.

Endnotes

CHAPTER 10

[1]*Newsweek*, (1 May 1978), 53.

[2]Virginia Stem Owens, *Wind River Winter* (Grand Rapids: Zondervan, 1987), 16.

[3]John E. Todd, ed., *John Todd: The Story of His Life* (New York: Harper and Brothers, 1876), 35–37.

[4]Nicholas Wolterstorff, *Lament For a Son* (Grand Rapids: William B. Eerdmans, 1987), 13.

[5]Ibid., 51.

[6]Mrs. Charles E. Cowman, *Streams in the Desert* (Grand Rapids: Zondervan 1963), 21.

[7]Owens, 220.

[8]Henri J.M. Nouwen, *A Spirituality of Waiting: Being Alert to God's Presence in Our Lives* (Notre Dame, Ind.: Ave Maria Press, 1985).

[9]Herbert Lockyer, *Dark Threads the Weaver Needs* (Old Tappan, N.J.: Fleming H. Revell, 1979), 122–123.

[10]Owens, 79.

CHAPTER 11

[1]Oswald Chambers, *My Utmost for His Highest* (New York: Dodd, Mead and Co., 1935), 129.

[2]Susan L. Leizkes, *When the Handwriting on the Wall is in Brown Crayon* (Grand Rapids: Zondervan, 1981), 16.

[3]Robert J. Hastings, "The Station" (98 Laconwood, Springfield, IL 62703)

[4]Elisabeth Elliot, *Shadow of the Almighty* (San Francisco: Harper & Row, 1958), 160.

[5]C.S. Lewis, *A Grief Observed* (New York: Bantam Books, 1961), 79.

[6]Philip Schaff and Arthur Gilman, eds., *A Library of Religious Poetry* (New York: Funk & Wagnalls, 1889 Dodd, Mead & Co.) 7-8.